Longman sociology of education

Educational opportunity and the home

Longman sociology of education

Educational opportunity and the home

Gordon W. Miller, B.A., Ph.D.
University of London Institute of Education

Foreword by Lady Plowden, J.P.

Longman

LONGMAN GROUP LIMITED
London

*Associated companies, branches and
representatives throughout the world*

© Longman Group Ltd 1971

First published 1971

ISBN 0 582 32453 X *cased edition*
ISBN 0 582 32454 8 *paper edition*

*Printed in Great Britain by
Hazell Watson & Viney Ltd, Aylesbury, Bucks*

To
Tamara, John, Sonya, Paul
Elizabeth and Tanya

Contents

Contents

Foreword

In 1964, following much earlier research on the effect of social class on the educational achievements of children, a National Survey was made of 'Parental attitudes and circumstances related to school and pupil characteristics'—its aim, to see how much parents influence their children's achievement at school. The results suggest that parents' *attitudes* to the education of their child were of prime importance and that 'parents' occupation, material circumstances and education explain only about a quarter of the variation in attitudes. . . . Parental attitudes appear as a separate influence because they are not monopolized by any one class. Many manual workers already encourage and support their children's efforts to learn' (*Children and their Primary Schools*). One additional sentence was omitted, that not all non-manual parents successfully provide the background to 'encourage and support their children's efforts to learn'.

Dr Miller, in his research described in the following pages, has implicitly accepted the additional sentence and has set out to look at the relationships within the family to see if those factors can be isolated which contribute positively or negatively to the academic success of a child, irrespective of social class. His findings are, I believe, of great interest to educationalists, social workers and parents alike. Those who have watched families and noted the success, semi-success or failure of the children will recognize families they know in the picture which emerges of the democratic and disciplined family in which children grow up with confidence in their own ability and culture; in contrast, the family where parents, in a lesser or greater degree, always know best and subtly undermine the inborn confidence of the growing child, an attitude so often associated with material and cultural deprivation.

In all developed countries there is concern about those children who do not develop their full educational potential, particularly in the families of manual workers. It is recognized that children are unequal, even by the time they reach school, by reason of the inter-action of heredity and environment. In this country it is at present hoped to achieve more equality at the primary stage by the pro-vision of nursery education in educational priority areas, and at the secondary stage, by a comprehensive system. The importance of the early years in the development of a child is widely accepted; but we still only pay lip service to the part that families can play in the education of their child and have neglected their role in the crucial first years, setting the pattern for the years to come.

Potentially parents are the most natural and cheapest teachers of all, but being a good parent does not necessarily come with parent-hood. Dr Miller's final emphasis is timely, on the need to support the immense sums of money at present spent on our educational system by small sums on giving parents professional advice on family rela-tionships. There is ample evidence that parents from all classes are anxious to learn. Perhaps I may quote the example of a coloured grandmother in Los Angeles, helping voluntarily in a nursery for deprived children. In reply to my question as to what help it was to her she replied: 'I listen to the teachers talking to the children and I learn how to talk in the same way. Last night me and the child (*sic*) went out and looked at the moon and talked about it.' Here was the beginning of a relationship with a learning potential for the child.

A greater interaction between parent, child care professional and child could lead to a greater number of children gaining more from their schooling than they do at present. Teachers cannot educate unaided. Dr Miller indicates the kind of relationship which more knowledgeable parents could provide within their own families to the benefit of their children's education.

BRIDGET PLOWDEN

Introduction

In recent years in Britain there have been several large shifts in government policy on education and in assumptions in the public mind. The major shift has been towards a strong emphasis on comprehensive education at the secondary level. Another has been in the acceptance of the concept of educational priority areas which should be singled out for special provision—positive discrimination. A further shift has been towards a deliberate fostering of the involvement of parents in the children's education.

People with differing philosophies, from Lord James of Rusholme to Sweden's former Minister for Education, now Prime Minister, Olof Palme, Torsten Husén, doyen of Sweden's educational research, and Jerome S. Kagan of Harvard University, agree on one thing: *that school reorganization is not enough.*

Lord James has been cited as follows:

The effectiveness of Britain's education depends on its being supported by the family. . . . However equal we make educational opportunity, however much we improve our schools, their influence is far from predominant when compared with that of the home. It is impossible to talk of equality of opportunity between the child from the good home with books and music and rational conversation, and the child from the overcrowded tenement with feckless or indifferent parents.[1]

Olof Palme has said: 'It is an illusion to believe that our (Sweden's) children have equal opportunity when starting school. We shall have to make that illusion a reality.'[2] And Husén: 'You have to influence ambition in classes with a low level of ambition to get real equality.'[3]

[1] *The Times Educational Supplement*, 10 October 1969.
[2] *Ibid*, 10 October 1969.   [3] *Ibid*, 26 December 1969.

Introduction

Kagan[1] in his reply to Jensen[2] in the *Harvard Educational Review* cites new studies which suggest that part of the perceived inadequacy of lower class children may derive from styles of parent–child interaction. The research reported in the present volume was directed towards the same problem as experienced by British school children. The detailed findings bear out those reported by Kagan in the United States.

What is not clear is what remedies may be found that will enhance equality through educational opportunity, apart from school reorganization which, on its own, is held to be inadequate.

This volume cannot suggest all the remedies, but it is hoped that the findings from the research described in it will provide at least a modest contribution to the solution of this problem.

[1] Kagan, J. S. (1969)—'Inadequate Evidence and Illogical Conclusions', *Harvard Educational Review* 39:2.

[2] Jensen, A. R. (1969)—'How much can we boost IQ and Scholastic Achievement?' *Harvard Educational Review* 39:1.

Acknowledgements

The help of a number of people is gratefully acknowledged. I am particularly obliged to the following: Professor Roy Parker of University of Bristol Department of Social Work and Administration, formerly of London School of Economics, was extremely helpful with his sensitive understanding of the research problem and his support throughout. Thanks are due to Professor Hilde Himmelweit for her help, and to Dr A. P. Sealy for his meticulous supervision of the statistical analysis; to A. H. Hendrickson and P. O. White of the Institute of Psychiatry for allowing the use of their FA 5 Factor Analysis Program, and particularly to P. O. White for his guidance on the factor analysis procedures.

The computing staffs at LSE, Imperial College and University of London Institute of Computer Science gave considerable help; and the University of London Central Research Funds (Irwin Fund) contributed a sizeable sum towards the costs of the research.

Mr Pascal, formerly Chief Education Officer, Enfield, and Mr Chamberlain, formerly Chief Education Officer, Ealing, who is now on the staff of James Cook University of North Queensland, were most helpful in providing access to the sample of schools and children. The research could not have started without their positive help and interest. To the headmasters and children in the schools I am also indebted for their willing cooperation in providing the data.

Finally, I should like to thank Lady Plowden for her encouragement and interest in the publication of this volume, and Sir Cyril Burt for his sympathetic and constructive comments on the manuscript.

G. W. M.
June 1970

Part I

The problem and its background

1

The problem

'It might be made of marble, Sir, but it would still be a bloody
school.' This statement exemplifies a common attitude among groups
of children whom education fails to reach. The boy who made the
statement, cited in the Newsom Report (1963), was a member of the
kind of working-class family against whom the British educational
system is sometimes said to discriminate. Does the system discriminate against such children? The answer is surely yes; but that is
really only half the answer, and it would be simpleminded to ignore
the fact that the social groups from which such children originate
unwittingly discriminate against themselves. The hostility towards
education felt by such groups is also often conscious and overt, and
educational priority areas discussed in the Plowden Report on
Primary Education[1] will have a high concentration of people who
reject education in the terms suggested by the above statement.

In identifying educational priority areas and their special needs,
obvious measures suggest themselves, such as providing more money,
schools and teachers; but whatever is done, account will have to be
taken of further underlying reasons for the rejection of school and
learning by children and their parents, and the failure of others,
despite strong motivation, to make full use of such education as is
offered. Some of the factors which are considered to influence school
learning are: social class, peer relations, language, emotional disturbance, anxiety, poor or inadequate self-concepts, level of aspiration,
lack of curiosity, lack of love, acceptance and warmth, harshness of
discipline, child-centredness, democracy, dominance and submission,
family discord, sex role identification. There are numerous other
variables associated with school achievement and educational devel-

[1] Areas in which there is much poor attendance and truancy, poverty-poor
housing and overcrowding and other forms of deprivation.

opment, some of which will be mentioned in the section on previous research which follows in the next chapter.

The main hypothesis in this study is that a child's personality, motivation and educational opportunity are gradually formed by the kinds of relationships a child has with the people who are important to him. These relationships start from birth. During the formative years of a child's life up to age eleven, constellations of motivation, interests and attitudes develop which will have a direct bearing on his educational development. These constellations, syndromes or factors are identifiable and their patterns can be plotted. It is a purpose of this book to demonstrate this.

The relationships which are the raw material of the child's motivations and interests are chiefly those he has had with his mother, father, other adult figures, and his siblings in the home environment. His relationships with his companions (or peers) in his neighbourhood and at school also have some influence, and the attitudes of his parents to school and learning and teachers will also be reflected in his aspirations and his motivation to learn.

The situation of the socially underprivileged child in school is not a new subject for research, though precise identification has yet to be made of the promoting and inhibiting aspects of home background which may explain gifted scholarship, failure and average performance. This is a question of motivation and how from the earliest years of a child's life environment can affect motivation. As Wall (1962) has pointed out, and as psychologists and educators are well aware, motivation is among the most difficult and obscure of all the theoretical and practical issues in general and educational psychology. Habits of curiosity and openness of mind are important factors in learning, and emotional blocks are generally known to be associated with inability to learn certain subjects. This is often thought to apply particularly to the learning of mathematics. It would equally appear that children's learning of other subjects is prevented by failure to develop habits of curiosity and a desire for knowledge, and that this failure stems from habits of mind the child has been allowed or encouraged to have in his family situation from the earliest years. If such habits of mind are discouraged in early childhood it is easy to see intuitively that they will be difficult if not impossible to bring out in the school situation. This would seem to be of greater direct importance than social class, though there may well be some association between the characteristics of home which affect learning and social class.

Highly significant correlations of the order of 0·30 to 0·35 are usually found between social class and academic achievement. Despite their consistency and size, correlations of this magnitude account for, at most 12 per cent of the variance in achievement leaving nearly 90 per cent to be accounted for by other factors. Furthermore, 'social class' is merely a general concept and cannot of itself explain differences in educational development.[1] It is essential to look closely at and beyond social class in seeking explanations and solutions.

Three questions arise :

1. What social factors other than social class account for variation in educational attainment?
2. Do these factors correlate as highly with social class as they do with achievement? Put another way, are those factors which promote educational achievement to be found only in middle-class families? And are those factors which retard school performance only found in working-class families?
3. What is the precise nature of the most influential factors in the child's social background which motivate for achievement in school regardless of social class?

Since the passing of the Education Act 1944, which was designed to enable every child to have the education appropriate to his 'age, ability and aptitude',[2] it has been found in many researches that working-class children in particular are unable, for some reason, to make full use of educational opportunity, that middle-class children stay at school longer, are over-represented in grammar schools (Glass, 1954), and in universities, colleges of advanced technology, and colleges of education (Jackson and Marsden, 1962).

[1] It must be realized, of course, that the purely occupational index of social class is a crude device. It does not take into account those other important indices of social class, wealth (capital) and power, though it does take into account prestige ascribed to the occupation, which is itself an important index.

[2] Education Act 1944, Sections 36 and 37, *passim.*

There is evidence (Douglas, 1964) that these effects are influenced by the homes of the children from their earliest years, so that by the end of primary school if not well before, children have had their educability largely determined. Douglas found that children are sometimes placed in low streams because they appear to be poor material for A streams. Decisions on streaming are sometimes partly based on the criterion of the children's speech, dress and general demeanour. All of these favour the middle-class child, possibly because teachers tend to be of middle-class origin or outlook. But middle-class parents do not all equally promote the educability of their children or their intellectual development. Wiseman (1964a) has said: 'Blanket terms such as middle-class and working-class conceal large differences. Within those classes are variations larger than exist between classes, particularly in attitude and ambition.' The question how precisely parents can facilitate their children's intellectual development and educability is not yet answered.

Freeburg and Payne (1967) of the Educational Testing Service, Princeton, have summarized a careful selection of the literature dealing with child-rearing practices that influence cognitive development, and claim that educators still do not have any adequate answer to a parent who asks specifically, 'What can I do during my child's pre-school years to improve his learning ability or intelligence?' Similarly we do not have an adequate answer to the parent who asks the same question relating to a school child of any age, except suggesting 'maximum environmental enrichment'. More adequate and detailed outlines of a proper answer are just now beginning to emerge.

The President of the Educational Testing Service in his 1965–66 Report has written of the need to focus on the early years if we are to improve educational opportunity at all levels. Citing the research of Hebb, Piaget, Bruner, Vygotsky and others he concludes that learning ability or intelligence is largely the result of interaction of the child and his environment. But a 'rich environment' is not easily defined. The questions remain: Just how can educators and parents best go about facilitating intellectual development in the early years? Specifically what factors are most likely to influence development? What forms of stimulation maximize cognitive growth and the taking advantage of educational opportunity? And at what age do some children become 'allergic' or resistant to education, and why? These questions are of vital importance to policy. How can we feel confident that raising the school leaving age will fully serve the interests of children unless we have answers to such questions? When we know some answers we can begin to set about involving children and parents in making fullest use of educational opportunity.

There has in the past been a mistakenly held idea among laymen that intelligence was fixed and entirely dependent upon innate endowment.[1] It was assumed that if a child had the requisite measured intelligence, he would be successful academically. This concept of intelligence is quite contrary to those of Binet (1909), Piaget (1947), Hebb (1949), Vernon (1960), and Burt (1965).[2] Intellectual development is determined by the interaction between innate endowment and environmental influences. Burt has stated that 'what can be observed or measured are never the original genetic tendencies themselves, but only the results of their interaction with various pre-natal and post-natal conditions'.[3] Exactly what constitutes an optimal environment has not yet been thoroughly studied, although several workers have pointed out the need for studies to discover the main influences, e.g. Himmelweit (1955) and Floud, Halsey and Martin (1956). Husén (1966) has stated:

A large body of research has shown that students (from working-class families and some categories of agricultural families) are greatly under-represented in secondary academic schools. This is the case in all countries of Europe, as well as the United States. In France, for example, until recently only one-eighth of the student population came from working class homes who form two-thirds of the nation's families.

[1] For a layman's view of the controversy see, e.g. *The Times Educational Supplement*, 2 December 1966, p. 1367. This controversy seems to be resurrected about every five years in the educational press by some individual who has not read Burt and others thoroughly.

[2] See Vernon (1958) for a contradiction of this view and a clarification of the present position.

[3] Cf. *The Times Educational Supplement* (letter), 17 September 1965; also numerous books and articles.

Husén also stated that even in the USSR, where ideology and deliberate policies are meant to be aimed at achieving a classless society, 60 per cent of the enrolment in Moscow's upper level schools has been recruited from the intelligentsia and the bureaucracy, and only 40 per cent from the homes of manual workers and farmers, though the latter form the greater proportion of the population.[1]

Blomqvist's study (1958) of Swedish secondary school children, showed that the home's cultural standard ranked with scholastic ability as a determinant of success in school. Another study, by Moberg (1951), showed that the social class origins of Swedish undergraduates were roughly the same from 1910 to 1943. The same has been true of Britain from pre-war days to the present. The work of many authors thus suggests the need to study closely the precise nature of the social class variable and the manner of its relation to academic performance at each educational level.

In the review of the literature, reference will be made to studies of anxiety, social class, cultural characteristics of the home, need for achievement, and the relation of each to achievement. Studies of anxiety have produced conflicting findings (see Reed, 1960). Some researchers claim that successful children may be more anxious (Davis, 1955) while others have found this to be characteristic of unsuccessful children (e.g. Hallworth, 1961). Studies of university students yield similar conflicting results. It may be that more consistent results would be achieved by researchers if questions were asked about the specific areas of anxiety which concern the successful as opposed to the unsuccessful.

It should be possible to discover some other characteristics of environmental interaction which are shared in common by successful children of different class origins, and some of those shared by the unsuccessful. Clearly some middle-class homes produce low achievers and some working-class families produce high achievers, yet of all references so far consulted, few have reported attempts to penetrate beneath the conceptual layer of social class to the dynamics of children's real life situations.

In Professor Glass's introduction to *The Home and the School* (Douglas, 1964) his concluding remarks included the following:

[1] Speech to Supreme Soviet by N. Krushchev, cited by Husén (1966).

8

Educational change will have to concern itself positively with efforts to involve children and young people in the process of learning and discovery. Dr Douglas rightly emphasizes that more research will be needed here, and not least into the means of intensifying the intellectual stimulus of the environment in the pre-school and early school years . . . and in attempts to secure a more effective collaboration between the teacher, parent and the child.

Floud, Halsey and Martin (1956) long ago pointed to the need for investigation into the precise nature of the hindrances placed by home background in the way of educating working-class children. They considered that, in the long run, the problem must be seen as part of the broader question of the interaction of homes and schools generally, and the influence of the home, whatever social level, on the educability of children. 'With the expansion of educational opportunity and the reduction of gross economic handicaps to children's school performance the need arises to understand the optimum conditions for the integration of school and home environment at all social levels.'

To regard mere academic failure as the whole of school failure is a limited view. Education is concerned with teaching people how to live and not merely to pass examinations. Some educators would say that education is primarily for teaching people to live and that passing examinations is a secondary aim which is incidental to the first. It is argued here that academic success is complementary to the more general aims of education, which include that of educating people to function well as individuals in society.

A basic assumption in the present study was that the two are interdependent and complementary. This was in fact demonstrated in the study. Academic achievement seems to go with social adjustment: it is often seen in schools that clever children are more popular, or that popular and well adjusted children get the best marks. It is assumed that a child who is successful academically generally has more chance of being effective individually and in society than one who is not successful. Limited academic attainment nearly always imposes some limit on the social effectiveness or competence of the individual.[1] Academic failure, therefore, may

[1] White (1959) discusses forms of behaviour which have to do with effective

9

be regarded as relevant to social failure. While not intending to disregard the importance of social failure in itself, the problem was viewed primarily as one of academic rather than social attainment. There are good reasons for using this narrow concept.

For the individual, academic failure generally entails economic loss because future occupational opportunities will most likely be confined to a few small steps at the bottom of the ladder.[1] It also limits social mobility.

Abrams (1964) emphasized the importance of academic attainment as an agent of social mobility :

A generation ago those who were critical of large inequalities of income concentrated their attack on inherited wealth; it is arguable [from evidence he cited regarding education related to income] . . . that today differences in educational background play a comparable part in creating inequalities of income.

Wall (1955) has described another aspect of the problem of low academic achievement. He states :

Many delinquents who are not markedly subnormal in their intellectual ability are found to be retarded educationally. Not all dull and subnormal children become delinquent; nor do the maladjusted or retarded; nevertheless, schools which make no provision to help those who fall behind for any reason, offer little satisfaction to a considerable group of children from among whom many delinquents are recruited.

Roucek (1965) produced some rather alarming statistics and comment further to this point. He writes :

Teenage unemployment [in the U.S.] is causing widespread concern, not only because of its considerable magnitude, but also because it has been increasing so spectacularly. The present one in six jobless rate for teenagers compares with only about one in ten as recently as 1958. The rate

interaction with the environment and places them under the general heading of 'Competence', to which Webster gives as synonyms capability, capacity, efficiency, proficiency, skill.

[1] What is educational opportunity? In the *Annual Report* (1965–66), of the Educational Testing Service, Henry Chauncey, its President, wrote, 'Education must be viewed as something broader than the school system. . . . Today we recognize that "opportunity" in a thoroughly unfavourable environment is no opportunity at all.'

among unschooled, unskilled dropouts who constitute roughly half of today's job seeking youths is one in three, up from approximately one in eight only five years ago. The dropouts [and among these he includes those who leave school at the compulsory minimum age of 16] have indeed a bleak employment future before them. Over the past ten years [he was referring to the years 1953–1963], with overall employment steadily expanding, jobs for those without high school education had declined by 25 per cent. . . . Of 4,322,000 unemployed in 1963, about two-thirds were people who failed to complete high school, many lacked even the meagre education to pass the qualifying tests for the government re-training programme.

As the British economy develops, the need for all possible education for adolescents and adults may assume the same importance as in the USA.

It is possible that a sense of frustration is engendered when a bright or normal child fails to achieve at the level of which he feels capable. Frustration can promote aggression, and it may be that in the children to whom Wall referred this aggression sometimes precipitates delinquent behaviour.

There is a further reason for focusing primarily on academic attainment. Frequent references are made to the problem of how to discover, encourage and make the best use of intellectual talent since this is one of the principal resources of a nation. American textbooks sometimes refer to this aspect of the problem (de Haan and Havighurst, 1961, Getzells and Jackson, 1962). Havighurst *et al.* (1962) considered that at least half of our best human material is not developing to anywhere near capacity, and Wall (1955) cited evidence that in the UK, of 1500 junior school children of superior ability more than half were two years retarded in reading comprehension, one-third were two years retarded in arithmetic, and three-quarters were two years or more retarded in spelling, as compared with their mental ages. Such a situation constitutes not only a loss to the economy of a country, but also means a diminution of the intellectual and general development of children and their life chances.

In the present investigation, a wide sampling of children's social and emotional activity was attempted. It would have been ideal if the totality of children's environments could have been studied.

Research confined to fewer and more specific variables might have been considered more scientific. This study was designed in full awareness of such criticism. It was discounted for two reasons. First, the purpose was to map out some main areas of social environment which would help in exploring achievement and intellectual development. If the study were confined to a few variables, that purpose might have been vitiated from the start, since the really important factors might have been missed. Second, there was no wish to be one of those to whom Whitehead (1933) referred : 'Clear-sighted men . . . who are so clearly wrong (and) ignore everything which refuses to come into line.' For these reasons a deliberate effort was made to bring as many variables as possible within the scope of the study.

2

Previous research

The literature of the social correlates of scholastic achievement has been largely concerned with easily observable and measurable aspects of social class. It is now well established that effective use of educational opportunities is limited for the child or adolescent belonging to a working-class family and enhanced if he is a member of a middle-class family, especially if it is a professional one. The aim of this study was to explore several possible kinds of explanations for this class bias including family and other social relationships, developmental tasks and anxiety. Previous research[1] is now reviewed under four headings: (1) Social class studies; (2) Anxiety studies; (3) Child–adult relations; (4) Developmental tasks.

Social class

Early studies by Burt (1937) suggested that environmental variables, such as poverty, population density, family size, poor health and inadequate general knowledge were the aspects of low social class which encouraged backwardness in school. Since those days there have been many changes in society making it possible for several of these to be reduced in importance. Poverty, poor health, and inadequate general knowledge would seem to be less intractable problems than thirty years ago, yet the problem of backwardness is still a serious one.

Himmelweit and Whitfield (1949) studied data of ten thousand army recruits, and found a high correlation between social class as judged by occupation and intelligence as measured by a short verbal

[1] There is, on the whole, agreement between American and British research findings, except, in places, in relation to anxiety. No attempt has been made here to distinguish sharply between the two countries.

test. Considerable overlap was found between the classes, the top class in intelligence (school teachers) overlapping with the bottom class (labourers). This overlap probably reflected the unequal educational opportunity that existed at that time, when people of high ability were denied the access to education and occupations for which their ability would have qualified them. It is possible that less overlap, and consequently a higher correlation, between class and intelligence would be found today since the use of tests of intelligence has tended to select candidates for education and occupations more on the basis of ability.

However, a study by Havighurst (1962) in the United States shows the persistence of this social class bias and that children of high social class tend to have high intelligence test scores. The parents of the top 37 per cent in social class were found to have 65 per cent more children with intelligence ratings above 110 than would have been expected. The upper 10 per cent in social class produced 80 per cent more children in this intellectual class than would have been expected. By contrast, the parents in the lowest social class group produced only 40 per cent of the number of children with IQs above 110 that their numbers would have suggested.

Furneaux (1961) has cited evidence in England of the strong correlation between fathers' occupational level and children's academic success. At primary school the proportion of children from white-collar families to those of unskilled fathers was 16 : 10. This proportion increased with each rise in educational level. In supported grammar schools it is 63 : 10; in the sixth forms of these schools it became 370 : 10; at university level it rose to 620 : 10. Furneaux attributed these proportions to the superior performance of professional workers' children in academic tests, and the greater willingness of both parents and children in this group to pursue educational goals. Kelsall in 1963 commented that this trend, though less pronounced, was still a serious matter to be reckoned with. The English maintained grammar school is apparently not markedly more successful as a social melting pot than it used to be, and he made a plea for more research to establish the factors involved in order to pave the way for appropriate social and educational measures.

Some evidence has been produced showing the importance of the cultural as well as the economic level of the home in relation to educational attainment. Campbell (1951) studied a large sample of secondary school children and their homes to see how much the cultural characteristics of the home influenced their school work. Among the aspects he studied were the access children had to music and other hobbies in their own homes; the kinds of books, newspapers, journals and radio programmes received in the homes; the presence of pictures; how often the children were taken to such cultural events as ballet and concerts; and the attitudes of the parents to education. His findings showed that these aspects of the home background seemed appreciably to affect success in secondary school. Children who performed in their school work above expectations tended to come from the more cultured homes, and those who performed below expectations came from culturally inferior homes. Campbell claimed that if cultural support of the home were taken into account, inaccuracy in selection procedures could be reduced by one-third.

Improvement of selection procedures is not the only matter that deserves consideration. There is a ceiling to efficiency in selection for higher education as Himmelweit (1965) has pointed out. The same applies to selection at the age of eleven. Diminishing returns rapidly set in once a certain point of efficiency is reached, and the well-known 'backwash effect' in the years preceding the year of selection is undesirable. Moreover, however efficient selection could be made there would still be unpromising pupils who would have performed better a year or two later had they been given the chance, and the promising ones who do not fulfil their promise.

Campbell's study, with its conclusion that by taking the cultural standard of homes into account selection can be improved, says nothing about other more positive applications of the findings. If it were known precisely what aspects of cultural and social inferiority in the home inhibit school performance, it might be possible to help children with such handicaps to do better, by guidance procedures that have so far not been developed.

Arvidson (1956) made similar findings to those of Campbell in his study of 400 boys and 400 girls from seven secondary modern schools. His enquiry was concerned with non-intellectual factors including persistence, attitudes to school, sex factors, teacher competence, and social, economic and cultural aspects of the home. He found that economic and cultural features of the home were of greatest importance for English. Persistence and sex difference seemed to play little part. Arithmetic attainment was less culture-bound and the related variables in order of importance were intelligence, school, home conditions and teacher competence. By taking such aspects of the home into account he considered it was possible to improve predictions of how well children would achieve in English. Although his findings were not so conclusive regarding arithmetic, Arvidson claimed that most of the variance in English scores could be accounted for by the seven factors studied. Of these, the most important were socio-economic class and cultural level, intelligence, teacher competence and sex. For arithmetic, most of the variance could be accounted for by intelligence, school, home conditions and teacher ability. One might expect a high correlation between verbal and English tests, but in his study a non-verbal test (Jenkins No. 1) was used which makes his findings even more remarkable. Social class and the cultural level of families were more significant than intelligence. This is the most interesting finding in his study.

Fraser (1955) found that another aspect of home environment was more closely related to school progress than intelligence. In contrast to Arvidson and Campbell, she found that emotional and abnormal home relationships such as separations, divorce, presence of stepparent, parental discord and economic factors were more important than cultural and motivational ones. Schonell (1956) reporting the Unesco Conference on school standards and school failure held at Hamburg in 1956, stated that of the research discussed, all suggested that there was more school failure among children from families where there was disintegration and discord; but still more failure occurred among children from homes of low cultural level and education. Members of the seminar believed that this was related to the low expectations of parents in regard to the child's achievement and progress, and that this was more characteristic of working-class than middle-class homes. Schonell sees a close connection between this and the different experiences which children have at home of the spoken or written word. Impoverished language and communication lead to backwardness in spelling, reading and English, with consequent difficulty in making full use of formal learning experiences.

Blomqvist's work (1956) in Sweden is reported by Schonell (1956). Blomqvist compared a group of eighty-six secondary school pupils who had to repeat classes, with a similar group who were regularly promoted. He found statistically significant differences in favour of promoted pupils in that they more often came from homes where parents had clearcut plans for their further education, held positive attitudes towards the school and higher cultural standards, and provided a better emotional atmosphere with greater marital stability.

Halsey and Gardner (1953) compared middle-class and working-class boys in grammar schools. They found that middle-class boys tended to achieve better: the lesser achievement of working-class boys appeared to be related to working-class parents having less aspiration for their children and exerting less pressure on them. This applied more in large than small families.

Cultural standards, opportunities for verbal and literal stimulation and interaction, and language style are all clearly associated with social class. Numerous papers by Bernstein (1958, 1960) and a book by Lawton (1968) suggest that differences in linguistic codes account for differences in educational development among children.

Bernstein posited a restricted code which is employed more extensively by working-class families, and an elaborated code which is more used by middle-class families. The elaborated code is composed of a greater variety of subtle expressions. For the middle-class child this represents an initial advantage in education. According to Bernstein's theories one might suppose that not only has the middle-class child more tools of thought at his disposal, but that he can adapt them to educational use and achieve flexibility of thought and expression. He is capable of greater abstraction and more ready understanding of the materials and stimuli presented to him in school than the working-class child. By comparison, the working-class child starts schools with a limited and rigid set of expressions and tools of understanding which are less specific and more ambiguous. While they provide a useful and rich medium of expression when augmented with a variety of inflections and gestures, they are useful only in the child's own segment of society and are too ambiguous for fine differentiations of meaning.

This initial disadvantage with which the working-class child starts school can seldom be overcome except where the child is of unusual ability. This view is supported by Bossio's (1965) study of deprived children and her review of other studies. Riessman (1962), in his study of the culturally deprived child agrees that such children do not realize their potential because of formal language difficulties. He refers to this as the Achilles heel in the education of the working class.

Like Bernstein, he stresses the significance of the different kinds of language used by middle-class and working-class children. The one used by working-class children limits their learning in the school situation which usually tends to be middle-class in nature.

Further evidence of this has been produced by John (1963), who studied patterns of linguistic and cognitive behaviour in a sample of Negro children from various social classes. He analysed three major levels of language behaviour, labelling, relating and categorizing. Consistent class differences in language skills emerged between the Negro children of different social classes. Middle-class children surpassed their lower-class peers in the size of their vocabulary, higher non-verbal IQ, and in conceptual sorting and verbalization. Middle-class children were at an advantage over working-class children in tasks requiring precise and abstract language. John considers that 'opportunities for learning to categorize . . . require specific feedback or careful tutoring, and such attention is less available to the lower class child'. Vernon (1960) has also pointed out that children from middle-class, and particularly professional, homes hear richer and more accurate speech, thus tending to use a wider vocabulary than those from working-class homes.

Keller (1963) has reported some preliminary findings of a recent project of the Institute for Developmental Studies at New York Medical College. These represent another aspect of the report by John already cited. She describes the slum child's life outside school as being extremely restricted. In her study no child mentioned reading as a leisure activity, interaction with adults was minimal and spasmodic, only half had even one meal a day with an adult, and their self-esteem was very low. Keller considers that such children have a profound initial handicap in scholastic competition with middle-class children. They usually fail to learn the rudiments of verbal and intellectual skills. In homes where parents do not read to their children, it is not difficult to imagine how the lack of this kind of introduction to books and the wealth of knowledge they contain can be a permanent handicap in children's learning.

Research has shown how class differences are reinforced at each stage of the educational process. Douglas (1964), in a national study, demonstrated how a selective and reinforcing action operated in the majority of English schools where streaming by ability was used. Children seemed to have been selected for A streams early in their junior school careers, partly on the basis of their initial advantages in linguistic skill and other forms of expression, appearance and responsiveness to school stimuli. This encouraged them to improve, and, conversely, the tendency was for working-class children who had been assigned to lower streams to deteriorate. Having fewer success experiences, their initial handicap increased over the years as they proceeded through primary school. Jackson and Marsden (1962) also explained that streaming increased differences that were already present as a result of home conditions before the children started school. They showed that increasing proportions of middle-class children succeeded in each selection stage, compared with the diminishing proportions of working-class children and Hotyat *et al.* (1947) showed how the standard deviation in reading ability widens the longer children are at school. This means that the longer children are exposed to teaching the more unlike they actually become in their level of attainment. Hotyat found that between the ages of seven and ten the standard deviation for reading nearly trebled from seven months to nineteen months, suggesting that powerful influences outside school account for the increasing spread.

A different aspect of the force of social class differences is presented in the separate studies of Douglas and Jahoda. Douglas found a semipermeable barrier between the manual and the non-manual groups in British society. In his longitudinal study of a national sample of all the children born on one day in 1946, he found that in eleven years only 5 per cent moved up, and only 3 per cent moved down across this barrier. This is a striking example of the rigidity of English social class divisions, and demonstrates the strength of the influences that determine it.

When this study is associated with that of Jahoda (1951) the importance of these influences is confirmed. Jahoda studied secondary modern boys and girls in an industrial town, and found that a deep sense of loyalty to the working-class reference group existed. Boys identified with Class V on the Hall Jones index and tended to choose between only two trades as the most likely job alternatives. There was little tendency to widen the field of choice, and mobility would by these means be restricted. Girls were less specific in their choice of occupation, and were more likely to choose those which offered prestige and fellowship. Both girls and boys generally had little desire for upward mobility and stated firm preferences for their own group. Such close identification of school children with group and parental values suggest that similar powerful social class identifications operate for educational aspirations as well as occupational choice.

By contrast, in the USA, Riessman (1962) discovered that when parents of lower social class were asked what they missed most that they would like their children to have, 50 per cent of white and 70 per cent of Negroes specified education. This apparent discrepancy between American and English studies might be explained by the differences in aspirations for social mobility in the USA and England. If English parents had the same educational aspirations for their children as those in the USA, the semipermeable barrier to which Douglas referred might become more permeable and allow greater upward mobility.

Further evidence of the nature of the relation between achievement and social class has been discovered by Douglas (1964) and Porter (1957) in their separate studies. Douglas found that parental interest played a highly significant role in children's academic achievement and in their remaining at school. Although parental interest is closely tied to social class, it was also effective within social classes, while Porter's findings suggest some of the ways in which parental interest might produce the effect of maintaining children at school longer. Interviews with parents of grammar-school children revealed that this interest manifested itself in several ways. There was a positive correlation between staying on at grammar school and the standard of the parents' education, their attitude to education, the provision of a heated room in which the child could study, their atitude to school as a means of securing good job prospects, and their desire for their children to remain at school.

LSE studies by Himmelweit, Halsey, Oppenheim and Bene of 600 thirteen- to fourteen-year-old boys produced some similar findings. Using projective methods and open-ended and multiple choice items they found that middle-class children were more concerned about how well they did at school. This probably reflected close identification with their parents' ideas and interests because middle-class parents were found to supervise their children's school work and leisure closely, and were more concerned about school work than working-class parents. Jayasuria (1960) in a study of 273 children of the same age in secondary modern and grammar schools set out to evaluate the relation of social class and intelligence to different aspects of aspiration and achievement motivation. He found that middle-class grammar school children had higher achievement motivation than middle-class secondary modern school children. Maas (1955) found further evidence of the influence of factors associated with social class. Fathers of fourteen- and fifteen-year-old boys were interviewed, and middle-class fathers were found to be more concerned than working-class fathers about social status and had higher educational and vocational aspirations for their children.

Evidence of a different kind relating to the way social class affects educational outcome resulted from a study by Kemp (1954, 1955), who studied schools as well as children. Fifty mixed junior schools in London were assessed on forty-two attributes including siting, amenities, the staff and their ability and attitudes, morale, socio-economic status of the homes of the children, and size of enrolment. Correlations were made between these and the level of attainment of pupils in the final year junior or top primary classes. Kemp found that the main factors favouring attainment were intelligence, social class, large enrolment and good morale. School morale was favourably affected by the attitudes of the head and the staff, but also by higher levels of intelligence and the social class of the children's parents. Interest in school was correlated with intelligence and social class, and maturity of behaviour as measured by Kemp was closely related to social class. Social class appeared to have a greater influence on attainment than did the size of school classes.

Douglas (1964) throws a clearer light on this in his discussion of streaming in which he writes that 'children from well-kept homes who are themselves clean, well-clothed and well-shod stand a greater chance of being put into upper streams than their measured ability would seem to justify. Once there, they are likely to stay and improve their performance in succeeding years. This is in striking contrast to the deterioration noticed in the children of similar initial measured ability who were placed in lower streams' (p. 118). The effect of such a process taking place in schools must reinforce the effects of unsatisfactory homes because the child in this situation is deprived of success experiences in both places.

Douglas also found that the average measured ability declines with each increase in family size, especially in the manual working classes. In large families the possibilities of rewarding intellectual experiences, and of proper care and attention are diminished. That these are influential in the growth of intelligence is suggested by such workers as Hebb (1949), Piaget (1952) and Berlyne (1957). They see intelligent behaviour as being determined by central processes, but subject to modification according to experience. They have discussed in different ways how early experience is of crucial importance in determining the final level of ability and modes of response.

Hebb's work, although done with rats, seems relevant to the question of how social class might affect the acquiring of intelligence and attainment in intellectual tasks. He reared two groups of rats of the same strain. One group was reared in cages with limitations on opportunities for experience and no facilities for problem solving. The other group was reared in a very large cage with a great variety of stimulating objects and barriers which gave experience in finding devious routes about the cage. At maturity, he gave the two groups problem-solving tests. As expected, the ones reared in the free stimulating environment, the rats' equivalent of a middle-class home, scored higher than the restricted ones. He then gave both groups ten days of training and tested them again. It might have been expected that the rats reared in the restricted environment, the rats' equivalent of a poor working-class home, would then reduce the discrepancy between their own performance and that of the free group. The reverse happened. The free group actually increased their lead, demonstrating that they could gain more from extra training than could the restricted group. They were 'more intelligent' rats. They had known more success experiences in their early development. The experiment suggests very strongly that it was these early rewarding experiences that gave them the greater ability to benefit by further experience at maturity.

Jayasuria considered that the higher aspirational levels and higher achievement motivation which he discovered in middle-class children was related to the fact that the more intelligent children have greater interest taken in them, receive more rewards and are encouraged to do better. But it is equally possible to interpret this the other way, and to say that the intelligent behaviour develops out of the success experiences and the stimulation in early life of the middle-class child, in the same way that Hebb's rats experienced the equivalent, and as Piaget has found with children.

These ideas are not new. As early as 1909, Binet, when discussing intelligence, made the following statement which has much relevance today in studies of intelligence and attainment, especially those related to social class.

Some recent philosophers appear to have given their moral support to the deplorable verdict that the intelligence of an individual is a fixed quantity. ... We must protest and act against this brutal pessimism. ... A child's mind is like a field for which an expert farmer has advised a change in the method of cultivating, with the result that in place of desert land, we now have a harvest. It is in this particular sense ... that we say that the intelligence of children may be increased. One increases that which constitutes the intelligence of a school child, namely, the capacity to learn.

Evidence has been collected separately by Douglas (1964), Mulligan (1951) and Havighurst (1953), suggesting that early social class differences may have a permanent influence upon the advantage people take of educational opportunity. Of Douglas's national sample, 15 per cent of the children with IQs of 113 and over left school at the age of sixteen; of these 80 per cent were working-class children. Mulligan compared male students supported by veterans' educational benefits with those who received no financial help in their studies. He found only a slightly higher proportion of sons of farmers, semiskilled and unskilled workers among the veteran students as compared with non-veterans. This is interesting because it might have been expected that the availability of such grants would boost the proportions of these classes in the veterans' group to a higher level than in the ordinary college population. A further interesting finding was that the sons of skilled workers more often took advantage of veterans' endowments for college education than the sons of semiskilled or unskilled workers. Mulligan concluded that cultural factors were of greater influence than economic ones in the under-representation of the lower social class groups at university when opportunity had been equalized.

Havighurst studied the level of education in relation to social status of youth. He found that 41 per cent of young people in the upper quartile of intellectual ability came from the homes of manual workers, yet only 10 per cent had graduated from college. Havighurst also studied a cohort of boys and girls from the sixth grade until some of them went to college. Of fifty-three boys in the upper quartile of intellectual ability, nineteen went to college. Those who did not go to college came mainly from working-class homes, had average or below average school grades, a lower achievement drive and lower personality adjustment scores than those who went to college. Wall (1955), reviewing studies of the part played by social class and personality adjustment in school achievement, concluded that where there is a considerable discrepancy between the values emphasized at home and those at school,

The strains may become very great and seriously prejudice future development. . . . During pre-adolescent years . . . the process of building up an idea of one's self in relation to others is proceeding. It is largely from the attitudes of parents, teachers and other children that the sentiment of self is developed. Lacking any objective criteria for self evaluation, children are dependent on what they think others wish them to be or suggest they are. Hence markedly divergent attitudes . . . or conflict between home and school are likely to be reflected in incompatibilities in the child's own idea of himself, and may provoke emotional crises which issue in a disturbance of behaviour.

Such conflict between home and school is more likely to exist for working-class children when they attend schools staffed by teachers with middle-class attitudes. The disturbed behaviour to which Wall refers might be expected to manifest itself in poor school work even though the grosser manifestations may not be present.

To summarize, social (occupational) class has been found in many studies to bear a substantial inverse correlation with academic ability and attainment. This has been attributed to various factors associated with social class. Among these are the intellectually less stimulating world of the child from lower social class groupings; streaming according to teachers' conscious and unconscious evaluation of children whereby children who do not dress well and do not appear clean are sometimes placed in B and C streams; the restricted language code of working-class children which is inadequate or inappropriate for the communication of knowledge from teacher to pupil; the differing values of various social class groupings; and pressures involved in loyalty to peer groups who do not have any strong motive for school attainment.

Of these cultural standards, aspirational levels, opportunities for intellectual expression and language style are probably the most discussed attributes of social class which are thought by researchers to influence attainment.

Anxiety

'. . . the problem of anxiety is a nodal point, linking up all kinds of most important questions: a riddle, of which the solution must cast a flood of light upon our mental life' (Freud, 1960).

The drive concept has been used by psychologists making controlled laboratory experiments in conditioning and learning since

Pavlov. The concept is capable of a wide range of meaning, and the term may include anything from a physiological need to one that is acquired or learned such as the anxiety to please parents or peers, a need to achieve or general anxiety. Mowrer (1950), N. E. Miller (1951) and Farber and Spence (1953) see anxiety as an acquired drive that motivates learning of certain kinds of behaviour.

Learning psychologists have hypothesized that when these needs or drives are satisfied they become reduced, and it is said that the response or the action that brought about satisfaction is thereby rewarded and reinforced. As this process is repeated with a variety of stimuli and rewards, habit patterns emerge and the character of the individual begins to form. If the response is not rewarded or reinforced, it tends not to be repeated and becomes extinguished. However, the possibility of a curvilinear relationship must always be held in mind. This possibility has not been fully explored, and such a relationship could account for some of the ambiguity of findings in the field of anxiety to which reference is later made. It is also necessary to consider the comparative importance of specific areas of anxiety, the particular matters which cause concern to the child.

Learning psychologists have not so far been able to make a definitive statement about the role of anxiety in academic learning, although it is widely accepted, rightly or wrongly, that children in school pay better attention when a little anxiety is induced. It may be that anxiety is a basis of curiosity, as has been suggested by Dollard and Miller (1950), curiosity in its turn being a good precondition for learning. To try to understand the many apparent discrepancies in the literature which will be discussed, it is well to ask for each study if some relief of anxiety was perceived by the subjects in relation to the tasks performed. For if it was not, learning psychologists would claim that the task was not then reinforced, and learning would be unlikely to have taken place.

Whether or not anxiety in children is reduced following positive responses in an academic situation appears to be in part a question of social class. For example, a middle-class child's parents reduce his anxiety by rewarding his school achievement. A working-class child perhaps derives less satisfaction from academic achievement, because it is not so likely to be an aspiration of his parents. Any anxiety he has about learning is more likely to be sustained, thus creating negative attitudes to learning, or at least some unpleasant associations with it. According to some researchers a working-class child is more likely to be rewarded for very different responses. While his school learning might be minimal, other kinds of learning might be considerable, especially social learning of working-class values and patterns of behaviour.

Social psychologists, notably Davis and Havighurst (1952), have developed hypotheses which are similar in some ways to those of learning theorists regarding the role of fear or something more akin to anxiety, in the socialization of children. Striving for rewards, for the prestige and acceptance of the group, for status within the group, and striving to avoid deprivation, are manifestations of adaptive socialized anxiety. Such anxiety leads to striving because it can in this way be reduced to a more tolerable level. Davis (1947) has held that middle-class parents induce in their children a fear of not being loved if they fail to set themselves and achieve middle-class goals. By using shame and guilt as methods of discipline the children are made to introject the middle-class values of their parents. By introjecting their values the children cope with their anxiety at the prospect of losing their parents' love, and at the same time manage to retain it. Once the anxiety is developed and relegated to pre-conscious and unconscious levels, its power to motivate children towards middle-class goals can be strong. Davis hypothesized that such adaptive socialized anxiety pushes the middle-class child, especially in adolescence, to develop middle-class conventions of behaviour and modes of communication and to pursue higher standards in educational attainment than their working-class peers who have no such anxiety to achieve these goals.

Bronfenbrenner (1958) traces movements in theories of socialization in the past twenty-five years, and particularly since Davis (1947) made her hypothesis. After outlining the Davis hypothesis, he quotes Maccoby and Gibbs (1954) whose work seems to indicate contradictory conclusions because they found middle-class parents to be more permissive than working-class parents. This does not demolish the Davis hypothesis regarding the presence of middle-class anxiety, because anxiety can still be generated in a permissive home, even though the child might be less aware of it. Bronfenbrenner's argument includes much about the question of strictness which might be seen as promoting anxiety, as opposed to permissiveness as a minimizer of anxiety, and also includes discussion on the fostering of the drive to achieve. Although he does not discuss anxiety *per se*, he is concerned with the social components of the Davis hypothesis regarding modes of discipline which are said to cause anxiety. One of his conclusions is that middle-class mothers still expect their children to be more independent, more responsible and to progress further in school, but are now more tolerant of their children than in the past. This suggests that although middle-class children suffer greater stress in being pushed towards greater achievement than other children, this is done in a more permissive and accepting atmosphere which allays some of the conscious feelings of anxiety that might otherwise be present.

One aspect of Davis's statement about the function of anxiety in social learning is often disregarded. Anxiety, she suggests, is generated about different aspects or foci of the socialization process, in different social groups. She argues (1947), that whereas a middle-class child learns a socially adaptive fear of receiving poor grades in school, of being aggressive towards the teacher, of fighting, of cursing and of having early sex relations, the slum child learns to fear quite different social acts. His gang teaches him the fear of being taken in by the teacher, of being a 'softie' with her. To study homework seriously is literally a disgrace. Instead of boasting of good marks in school, he conceals them if he ever receives them.

The middle-class child thus has anxiety generated or relieved by making responses which are quite different from those of slum children. This might partly explain why the literature of anxiety and attainment is seemingly contradictory. If it is agreed that anxiety can have different foci as Davis suggests, it is not surprising that clashes occur in research findings. Different concepts and measures of anxiety, and attempts to measure certain kinds of anxiety, for example general anxiety as opposed to anxiety specific to certain situations, might also have contributed to different kinds of findings, and retarded the establishment of a clearly defined theory.

Lynn and Gordon (1961) have written about studies in one dimension of anxiety, neuroticism, as follows: 'The relation between neuroticism and attainment is evidently in considerable confusion. The English studies tend to suggest that the relationship is positive, and the American findings that it is negative.' These authors consider the relation between introversion and attainment to be more firmly established. Himmelweit (1960) found no evidence of greater overall anxiety or tension among middle-class children than in working-class children, despite many confirmatory findings of the greater pressures to which middle-class children are subjected. Middle-class children are held to be under greater direct pressure from their parents, and experience more rigid superego and introspectiveness in handling frustration. Himmelweit believes that the lack of evidence regarding supposed higher levels of anxiety in middle-class children is related to the far greater childcentredness of middle-class homes, and that pressures upon middle-class children are 'exerted in a protected cushioned environment (and) can be tolerated without undue anxiety'.

In reviewing the literature one is forced into discovering the diverse nature of anxiety, and to conclude that it is is possible to examine only a small number of aspects of it at one time, and generally in relation to a particular problem. The global concept of anxiety is elusive, perhaps almost meaningless. Possibly no one kind of anxiety is experienced by different kinds of individuals in their diverse situations.

In the review which follows anxiety will be discussed under these subheadings:
1. anxiety promoting attainment;
2. anxiety retarding attainment;
3. mixed findings in anxiety studies.

Anxiety promoting attainment
Vernon (1953) stated that a positive correlation was frequently found between academic attainment and emotional instability, and some research suggests that there is more anxiety and worry among pupils who get into grammar school than among those who do not (1957). Spiro (1958) made a study of a kibbutz in Israel, where it is

common for children to spend a great deal of time apart from their parents while the latter go to work on nearby farms and other enterprises. While most children spend a reasonable time with their parents, they are not all conscious of the family as a separate cohesive unit giving all the support they feel they need. Spiro noted that the more anxious ones attempted to reduce the anxiety of being inadequately loved by engaging in activites that would bring approval and prestige, by conformity, excellence in work and dedication to study. In a study of 618 grammar and secondary modern school boys, Bene (1957) found grammar school boys felt more guilt about parents, school and people in general, and had more negative attitudes than secondary modern boys. She speculated that these attitudes might be due to the fact that the parents and teachers of grammar school boys are more authoritarian. If her view were true, it might be assumed that they felt greater stress and possibly anxiety as a result : in any case the greater guilt suggests greater anxiety in the grammar school group.

Several other studies provide further evidence that anxiety enhances attainment. Yates and Pidgeon (1957) found that girls do better than boys in the selection examinations for grammar school, and Terman and Tyler (1954) that women achieve better academic results than men. Eysenck (1959) pointed out that women tend to be more introverted than men. Lynn and Gordon (1961) suggested that these studies together provide indirect evidence that introversion is correlated with academic achievement. Lynn (1955) produced evidence that anxious children tend to be good readers, and Gough (1946) found in sixth grade pupils a negative correlation between emotional adjustment and achievement, suggesting that maladjustment is associated with achievement. Lynn (1956) gave several tests of anxiety to eighty boys and girls in a junior school, and forty-five boys in a secondary modern school. All children were then given tests in reading and arithmetic, and the junior school children an additional test in spelling. He made a general finding that anxiety enhances attainment in these tasks. In a study linking anxiety with level of aspiration, Ausubel *et al.* (1953) tested high school students to see if the two were correlated. They found a significant positive correlation between anxiety and magnitude of academic aspiration.

Lynn and Gordon (1961) and Furneaux's (1956) studies made use of Eysenck's theory (1952, 1957) which posits four main dimensions of personality, neuroticism, introversion-extraversion, psychotism and general intelligence. Furneaux (1956) studied university students and found a positive correlation of both introversion and neuroticism with success in academic work. Lynn and Gordon studied sixty male university students in 1961 and confirmed some of Furneaux's findings. They found positive correlations between introversion and persistence, and between neuroticism and size of vocabulary. Subjects in the mid-range of neuroticism performed best in intelligence and educational attainments tests, but no significant overall correlation was found between neuroticism or introversion and intelligence. Finally they concluded that the optimal level of neuroticism for academic performance was in the region of half a standard deviation above the national average.

Anxiety retarding attainment

The foregoing studies suggested that attainment is better in persons who experience certain kinds of anxiety, especially introversion and neuroticism. However, there is other evidence that general anxiety, anxiety following frustration or failure in different tasks, and less easily identifiable forms of anxiety suggested by such symptoms as hostility, low level of aspiration and negative behaviour, have an inhibiting effect on learning. Wall makes the following statements :

The effects of the world war of 1939–45 with . . . the general disturbance of social and emotional security in which children lived are clearly reflected in a striking increase in retardation. . . . Learning in the strictly educational sense will not proceed satisfactorily if the child's emotional life is disturbed . . . stability and self-confidence lie at the root of the child's power to learn (1955). A great deal of evidence has accumulated in past decades which seems to show that school failure is closely associated with disturbances in the growth of personality. . . . Continuous failure is associated with lasting personality disturbances (1962).

The following studies provide considerable empirical evidence to support the hypotheses suggested in the foregoing statements. Laboratory studies of the effects of failure, frustration and stress are cited. Each experiment could be expected to produce anxiety in the sub-

31

jects, and they suggest a link with level of aspiration and how it is affected by success or failure.

Takano (1959) took a sample of ninety-two children and divided them into homogeneous sub-samples according to age and IQ rating, then gave them the simple task of constructing a mechanical toy. He then gave them further problem-solving tasks and picture puzzles. Those who had been successful in the first task (the least frustrated) increased their adaptiveness in the later tasks, and those who had failed became less adaptive. Effects of frustration were more directly studied by Sandin (1944), using two groups of high school seniors. One group was put under stress by faked poor results and a contemptuous attitude on the part of the experimenter. The other group was encouraged by faked good results and the pleasant attitude of the experimenter. In the frustrated group, perception of failure induced poorer performance, day-dreaming, passivity and inefficient attack on the tasks. By contrast, the encouraged group showed no symptoms of frustration or anxiety and attacked the tasks well. Two other studies produced similar findings. Sherman and Bell (1951) gave high school students a test in recalling words, and found that those who were successful in the first test did better in the second, while the failure group were less successful. Lantz (1945) gave nine-year-old boys Binet tests. When they were given similar tests later, the successful ones performed them better and showed more cooperation and persistence than those who had failed.

A further study by Rao (1954) shows the same effects of stress on aspiration in two groups of adolescent boys. The boys were set a motor task in which a steel ball had to be hit along a groove with a stick. Stress was imposed by manipulating the results and telling the subjects they had failed. They were encouraged to set themselves goals and were then thwarted by the false information of failure. Their level of aspiration at first decreased in direct relation to the duration of stress, then stabilized at a low level. Aspiration and performance scores both improved after the stress was removed. In another section of the experiment Rao was able to elicit three levels of performance, by manipulating three separate levels of suspense, in each of which something akin to mild anxiety was induced. Suspense was arranged by the presence or absence of information of importance to the subjects. Performance was low when results were not communicated to the subjects. It was medium when the goals were not stated. Performance was highest when the procedure was arranged so that first, the goal was stated; second, the task was performed; third, results were given to the subjects. This experiment illustrates the role of anxiety as posited in learning theory. When the subjects were kept in suspense we can assume some degree of anxiety was created by the ambiguity of the situation. When they were told the results reinforcement was effected by the reduction of the suspense (anxiety), in the manner suggested by Dollard and Miller (1950).

Other laboratory studies have confirmed the negative effect of anxiety on different tasks in varying situations. Gynther (1957) found that anxious subjects could not communicate well orally, Moldawsky and Moldawsky (1952) that anxious subjects did less well on a digit span test than non-anxious ones, and Mandler and Sarason (1952) found a tendency for low anxious subjects to learn better than a high anxious group in trials of the Kohs block design test and in mirror tracing and maze learning. In the latter study, however, Mandler and Sarason concluded that a moderate amount of anxiety encouraged better performance, because those with little anxiety improved when they were given a failure report between trials.

Another study relating to anxiety, level of aspiration and attainment was carried out by Clark, Teevan and Ricciuti (1956) with university students. The authors found that subjects who most feared failure, were, through anxiety, pessimistically denying themselves the possibility of goal attainment. For them anxiety had the effect of lowering their level of aspiration and their attainment was thereby limited. Havighurst *et al.* (1962) in the United States and Schonell *et al.* (1962) in Australia have both produced evidence suggesting that anxiety depresses attainment at university. Havighurst studied fifty-three boys in the top quartile of intellectual ability, nineteen of whom did not go to college. All nineteen had lower personality adjustment scores than those who went to college. Schonell *et al.* investigated the careers of 400 university students. They found some with IQ ratings between 125 and 134 who performed poorly, 40 per cent could not make normal progress while others with IQs as low as 105 to 114 were more successful. Of those who failed, 42 per cent complained of emotional problems. Schonell concluded that given a minimum level of intelligence, schooling and determination to succeed, and provided they had few emotional problems, students were able to complete their degree courses. Corroboration of these findings is found in Priestley's (1957) study of the mental health of university students in which he gives evidence of the 'spiralling interaction between high failure rates and high anxiety'.

In the more numerous studies of school children, findings are consistent with those of laboratory experiments and university studies. Hallworth (1961) studied eight groups of boys and girls from first and fourth years of grammar and secondary modern schools. Each group numbered 112 subjects and was divided by age, sex and type of school. Anxiety was measured by eight selfrating questionnaires, including tests of self blame, manifest anxiety, separation anxiety, emotional stability, and social and emotional introversion. He made predictions on the basis of Davis's (1947) theory of adaptive socialized anxiety, and generalizations from the work of Lynn (1956); in particular that grammar school children, being the highest achievers, would experience more anxiety than secondary modern school children. He found the reverse. Secondary modern children, the lower achievers, scored higher than grammar school children in every test of anxiety and its variants that was administered. His findings do not support the simple hypothesis that attainment correlates positively with anxiety. On the contrary, he concludes that 'if any assertion may be made regarding the general relationship of anxiety and attainment, it is that they are negatively correlated'.

Specific learning tasks have been affected less by low anxiety in other studies. McCandless and Castenada (1956) found that reading and arithmetic suffered more by interference from anxiety than simple mnemonic skills like spelling; and Waite *et al.* (1958) that subjects with low levels of anxiety could memorize numbers in a test situation better than highly anxious subjects. These studies are of special interest, because they involve exhaustive studies in hundreds of classrooms in the United States of the relation of test anxiety to IQ. Ninety per cent of their correlations have been negative. Gordon (1958) also found a negative correlation between anxiety and learning.

In school attainment, the deleterious effects of anxiety have been confirmed by Fraser's (1955) observations. Her studies of 408 Aberdeen children showed that for children with IQ ratings above 100, abnormal home background likely to cause emotional stress was more influential than IQ differences in affecting progress adversely at school. This finding is similar to that of Schonell in Australia cited earlier, concerning university students.

Other studies suggestive of this are the separate ones of Burns, Keller, Montgomery and Walsh. Burns (1949) reports that children of high intelligence being treated in a Birmingham clinic 'were unable to use their intelligence adequately because their mental horizons were too clouded by fears, inhibitions, currents of affect and anergia'. Montgomery (1956) noted that high school dropouts showed more hostility (possibly a symptom of longstanding frustration and anxiety) towards teachers, police and parents, than the students who were intending to stay in school until graduation. Keller (1963) found very low self-esteem among slum children, who are notably low achievers and usually fail to learn the rudiments of verbal and intellectual skills. Walsh (1956) found that bright low achievers were unable to express themselves freely and adequately, felt themselves more criticized, and perceived their environment as being more restricted than did the high achievers. This syndrome suggests that the low achievers experienced greater anxiety than the high achievers.

Mixed findings in anxiety studies

In the two preceding sections, a review of much of the literature has demonstrated that no definitive statement has been made of the way in which anxiety influences attainment. The evidence suggests that anxiety is a complex variable which influences people in different ways in different tasks and situations, and according to the level of anxiety usually experienced by the subject. Reed (1960) has referred to anxiety as the ambivalent variable and notes that it is not always clear what meaning some researchers attribute to the word. He points out that the commonest confusion over the concept, that is 'whether anxiety refers only to an immediate emotional discomfort or whether it implies as well a vague feeling of fearsome anticipation about the future'.

In the light of the psychoanalytic theory regarding anxiety and defence mechanisms which, according to Freud (1915, 1923, 1926, 1936, 1960), a person unconsciously uses to deal with anxiety, and which have the function of hiding its cause by relegating traumata to the unconscious, the possibilities of research into the effects of anxiety upon 'learning' appear extremely complicated. If Freudian theory is to be accepted, the question may logically be asked, 'How can a person report his most significant anxieties if they have become unconscious?' As May (1950) has put it, 'the person in severe anxiety may be driven to deny the existence of the apprehension—not by caprice or by any uncooperativeness, but simply as a function of the severity of the anxiety itself'. This suggests serious methodological problems which it is not the present concern to explore.

If the anxiety is so complex and elusive that admitted or manifest anxiety scales can sample only superficial anxiety, and if some anxieties are held to exist at one time in the conscious and at others in the unconscious, another partial explanation of the conflicting findings in this area might be indicated. It is possible for a very anxious person to admit little anxiety and for a less anxious person to admit more. In the following section, research is reviewed which illustrates the mixed effects anxiety can have on performance in different intellectual tasks. A variety of measures of anxiety have been used in the different studies, and it is possible that this partly accounts for some of the mixed findings. Whether the studies are of the laboratory type or concerned with attainment at school or university, one general pattern of variation can be traced—that different levels of anxiety seem to have different effects upon performance of simple and complex tasks.

Laboratory studies

In these studies there was a trend suggesting that highly anxious subjects were more 'conditionable' and able to learn quickly simple tasks requiring speed rather than thought, and less anxious subjects better able to comprehend and learn more complex tasks. For example, Farber and Spence (1953) selected the 20 per cent most anxious subjects and the 20 per cent least anxious from a large group of psychology students, using the Taylor Anxiety Scale. The low anxious were better in learning the stylus maze, but the high anxious were superior in eyelid response conditioning. Spielberger *et al.* (1958), with a sample of eighty-eight students using the same anxiety measure, found a significant relationship between anxiety and task difficulty. The subjects had to redraw designs that had been presented to them. The high anxious performed better in the easy tasks, but the low anxious were superior in the more difficult ones.

Chansky (1958) gave his subjects a reading test and found that the high anxious could read faster, suggesting again that anxiety facilitates performance where some motor coordination and some element of conditioning might be involved. However, the low anxious comprehended better, suggesting that anxiety inhibits performance in the more complex tasks which resemble educational attainment. Castenada *et al.* (1956) made similar findings with a group of fifth grade children, showing that anxiety has the same differential effects on children as on university students. His thirty-seven children had to learn combinations of light buttons to press in a certain order. Again the high anxious were more successful in the easy combinations, while the low anxious were superior in the difficult ones. Ausubel *et al.* (1953) have presented findings that show the same trend in a different way. Their subjects were asked to make ten trials on a maze test. The high anxious were inferior to the low anxious at first, but after ten trials there was no difference between the performance of the two groups. It seems that the greater acquaintance with the test situation in the latter part of the experiment brought about a lowering of anxiety in the high anxious as the experiment proceeded, and this facilitated performance where before it had been inferior under the drive of high anxiety.

These experiments, although a small representation of laboratory studies, clearly and briefly exemplify the different kinds of findings which are reported in this area. They confirm that anxiety varies in its effects depending upon its level and the kind of learning involved. They also suggest that high anxiety, although it facilitates simple tasks, reduces the span of attention, preventing a child from exerting the sustained effort necessary for academic success.

As in the laboratories, where no simple statement can be made about the role of anxiety, so it is in studies which are concerned with academic achievement in school and university. The findings seem confused in a general sense, but if a more detailed and sophisticated view is taken, trends can be seen which suggest the direction in which different levels of anxiety operate on different kinds of learning. For instance, the studies of Lynn (1957), Klausmeier (1958), Sarason *et al.* (1958), Sarnoff *et al.* (1959), *Frankel* (1960) and Kimball (1953) give different kinds of findings which illustrate the differences as they apply to school children. Lynn studied a mixed group of primary school children aged between seven and eleven, and secondary modern school boys with a mean age of fifteen, to investigate a syndrome of anxiety and good reading in conjunction with poor arithmetic. In the primary school group anxiety and good reading were significantly related to poor arithmetic, but there was no correlation for the secondary modern group. Lynn's original position was that general anxiety inhibits performance in arithmetic, but promotes good reading, but this was confirmed only in the primary school children. Biggs (1959) took a different view, that anxiety about arithmetic depresses learning of arithmetic but that 'number-anxious children, particularly girls, expend more effort in English in the attempt to find some security in their studies at school'. Sarnoff *et al.* found in England no association between test anxiety and attainment in the eleven-plus examinations, but in the United States they found a negative correlation between text anxiety and intelligence test scores. To explain this they hypothesized that some highly anxious individuals 'are able to compartmentalize their anxiety and divert it into behavioural channels which run parallel to the ongoing task'.

Sarason *et al.* (1958) found that high anxious boys, who incidentally are less common than high anxious girls, were less persistent and not so effective academically, but in girls there was no difference in performance for different anxiety levels. They explained that in a Rorschach study in which the same children took part, the high anxious boys showed more negative self attitudes than high anxious girls. They considered that high anxiety in girls acts as a strong motivation to achieve, whereas in boys it was more often associated with denigration of the self. Frankel (1960) investigated the anxieties of fifty pairs of achievers and under-achievers, and found that they were anxious about different things. The under-achievers were more anxious about their school work, and the achievers were more anxious about family quarrels and whether they would be able to make a satisfactory career in college or business. Kimball (1953) discovered that the anxiety level of under-achievers was not statistically different from that of normal achievers. Over-achievers showed more anxiety in Rorschach tests, but inferiority feelings were more common among the under-achievers, suggesting that feelings of inferiority inhibited aspiration, thus limiting the goals they set for themselves.

Further research by Lynn (1959), Grooms and Endler (1960), Broadbent (1958), Bendig (1960), Duff and Siegel (1960), and Alpert and Haber (1960), which have been concerned with university students have resulted in similar mixed findings. Lynn took the view that anxiety is too general a concept, being related to both introversion and neuroticism, and suggested they should be studied separately. However, in his 1959 study he concluded that even the relatively confined concept of neuroticism could have different effects in different situations and for different work. He concluded that at university and in the sixth form, although neuroticism is disorganizing in stress situations, this is more than compensated for by its facilitating effect in motivating for sustained work. Alpert and Haber noted something similar but took a different view. They considered five different anxiety scales and the direction of the effects of anxiety upon academic achievement in university students. They concluded by positing the existence of one form of anxiety which debilitates academic learning and one which facilitates.

The paradox in current research referred to by Cox (1956) and demonstrated in this review might be explained by these suggestions of Lynn and Alpert and Haber. Cox adds to these a further possibility, that high anxious subjects are not a homogeneous group, but are heterogeneous with respect to their different reactions to stimulation. Child (1954) has reviewed earlier studies of anxiety and learning and concluded that

as the task becomes more complex there is a tendency for high anxious subjects to show increasingly poor performance in comparison with low anxious subjects, and subjects with high test anxiety differ from those with low test anxiety in their habit of responding to anxiety which has been built up through their lives. High anxious subjects have habits of responding to anxiety which are incompatible with efficient pursuit of a complex task. Hence they do worse in situations which evoke anxiety, because these responses are irrelevant to the task. Low anxious subjects, on the other hand, lack habits of responding to anxiety with task irrelevant responses, so that anxiety-arousing instructions have as their main effect on these subjects an improvement of performance through increase in drive. . . . It would appear that response tendencies to anxiety must be taken into account.

There is another argument put forward by Easterbrook (1959) who thought that emotion (presumably including anxiety) always acts to reduce the range of cues received and utilized by the individual, similar to the notion of Sullivan (1947) who saw anxiety as causing a restriction of consciousness of what is going on in one's situation. Easterbrook claims that it 'is empirically determined that, when the direction of behaviour is constant, increase in drive is associated with a reduction in the range of cue use'. He argues that this effect of anxiety could be organizing or disorganizing, depending upon the behaviour concerned. Some tasks require response to a wide range of cues. Emotion (presumably including anxiety), by limiting the range of relevant cues received could thus limit performance in these tasks. However, in other kinds of tasks (these might include the more complex learning tasks), a greater number of cues are irrelevant and must be excluded if best performance is to be facilitated. When they are excluded emotion becomes channelled so that it exerts an organizing and motivating effect. It is possible that such a process takes place when a person pursues long-term academic goals.

To conclude this section it seems most relevant to cite at length the following statement by Reed (1960), which is a good summary of the major points suggested by the present state of research on anxiety and learning:

(*a*) Severe anxiety seems to depress learning.

(*b*) A mild degree of anxiety may function in a positive manner for some forms of learning.

(*c*) A very low level of anxiety may depress learning.

(*d*) Certain learnings may be independent of the anxiety variable.

(*e*) The nature of the learning criterion may account for variations in the effects of anxiety.

(*f*) The effects of anxiety may vary in relation to the strengths of other antecedent variables present.

(*g*) No one theory explaining human behaviour would appear to be sufficiently advanced to account for the variety of [learning] phenomena being reported.

The ambivalence of the anxiety variable in its effects on learning becomes more understandable when its complexity is emphasized. Three factors must be considered as regards anxiety. First is the notion of levels of anxiety, with different levels acting in a nonmonotonic pattern. Second is the affinity of the anxiety variable for other interacting factors, with these interactions changing the intensity and even the direction of effect. And third is the variation of effect in relation to different types of learning.

The principle of individual differences will be of particular importance to teachers who may wish to explore the possibilities of anxiety. Different abilities will determine how much can be demanded of a given individual before his anxiety becomes depressing rather than facilitating. Further, different student personality characteristics may also determine just how insecure the learning situation can become without developing undesirable concomitant effects.

Child–adult relationships

In reviewing the studies of social class and anxiety and their relationship to attainment and intelligence it has become apparent that underlying these variables are others which are less accessible to research and upon which not very much research has been done. The area of family relations in relation to attainment has been little studied as Morrow and Wilson (1961) have pointed out.

Many studies have stressed the importance of family relations, pointing to the need for this kind of research, in the realization that achieving behaviour is not something that arises in a vacuum. Wall (1962), has stated:

Parent child relationships . . . are fundamental to the pupil's whole development, and particularly to his ability to apply himself in school. . . . It is vital to know whether there is adequate security and love, whether the child is reared in an atmosphere of relative calm and understanding or whether he is the centre of tensions and consequent anxiety. . . . Records of child guidance clinics and educational guidance centres show that with intelligent pupils, adverse socio-emotional conditions in the home, particularly where basic psychological needs are not satisfied, are frequently the primary cause of maladjustment in the school situation. Although a pupil may show in school symptoms indicating something is wrong, it is only by careful analysis of the home situation that actual tension and frustrations are revealed . . . and of course not only the experiences, but their psychological significance to the child. . . . It is important to stress that the effect of parental attitudes and the general climate of his home on a child may be shown not only in the strictly educational acquisitions which he is able to make, but also in the growth of his ability to learn—his intelligence.

Himmelweit (1955) also has pointed to the comparative paucity of studies in this field, writing :

It seems that too many studies have concentrated upon external happenings . . . and have placed too little emphasis upon the emotional context in which they occur. . . . It would be important to map all regions in which tensions are aroused in the adolescents of the two classes— regions which may well differ from one another. . . .

Morrison and McIntyre, as recently as 1969, have said, 'We do not know . . . what accounts for the statistical relationship between parental attitudes and pupil achievements.' They cite a study which found that the average attainments of pupils in a group of schools selected by inspectors as having particularly good parent–teacher relations were *not* found to be significantly different from those of pupils in the representative sample of schools.

Symonds (1947) has expressed the view that the various degrees to which either parent gives, withholds, dominates, rejects, praises or punishes determine the type of personality formed [and presumably patterns of motivation for the many endeavours, including intellectual, to which an individual may aspire]. Crandall (1964) studied forty grade school children and their mothers and fathers by interview. He found that general parental behaviour significantly predicted the children's academic test performance. This was especially so in the case of mothers and daughters. Mothers of academically competent girls were less affectionate and nurturant towards their daughters than the mothers of less proficient girls. He also found that parental attitudes and interest in children's intellectual efforts had greater effect on daughters' achievement than sons'.

In early studies of intelligence and attainment it was held that innate mental capacity was all important because it was considered to be constant from birth. The work of Burt (1937) and Newman, Freeman and Holzinger (1937) seemed to substantiate this. Their famous twin studies suggested that about 80 per cent of IQ variation could be accounted for by heredity. While the presence of inborn differences must logically remain an unassailable fact, there has been a shift in recent years to the view shared by Burt (1947, 1955), that environmental variables are of greater significance than was generally conceded. The wheel has turned full circle to that rarely quoted statement of Binet (1909) cited on page 23, likening the child's mind to a field which can be cultivated to produce, under favourable conditions, more than would have been thought possible so long as the restricted view of inborn ability as a constant was held. Burt (1947), wrote in similar terms: 'The normal child is also frequently handicapped by his social background. . . . His future development will depend, not merely upon his innate mental capacity and temperament, but upon the interaction between his innate and slowly maturing endowment and the field of social forces in which [he] matures.'

After reviewing literature of the relation of experience to intelligence, Hunt (1961) concluded:

So long as intelligence was assumed to be fixed and development assumed to be predetermined, every effort was made to show that differential heredity alone could account for retardation and apathy. In the light of newer developments in both conceptualization and evidence, heredity, while it may still be an important factor, can no longer be assumed to have major responsibility for these differences.

Hebb (1958) has taken a very clear position which is closely in harmony with more recent thought in this area. He states:

Sometimes it is recognized that heredity and environment both affect intelligence, but the writer then goes on to say how important each is, for example, that 80 per cent of intelligence is determined by heredity and 20 per cent by environment . . . we must say that both are of 100 per cent importance : their relation is not additive but multiplicative. To ask how much heredity contributes to intelligence is like asking how much the width of a field contributes to its area. . . . It has been found repeatedly that cultural differences can affect intelligence test scores to a very marked degree . . . intelligence is the joint product of the physical and social environment.

Piaget (1947) earlier made the same point using different expressions. For Piaget intelligence is adaptation which proceeds through assimilation of selected stimuli from the environment and their incorporation into inner schemata already inherited or built up from past experience. He argued that the environment is indispensable to this development because environment partly determines what the child will assimilate into his schemata, merely by the presence or absence of certain stimuli.

Selection of stimuli to be incorporated into schemata is probably determined by the emotional tone associated with specific stimuli. In Hebb's (1949) experiment with rats to which reference was made earlier, it is significant that the ones reared as pets developed greater intelligence and were able to solve problems better at maturity than those which had no fondling. According to Erikson (1950), the child's basic trust in himself and the world about him originates in the oral stage of development. Erikson argued that emotional satisfaction from oral experiences in infancy helps to establish a strong self-concept or identity and self-esteem which gives him a sound base for future psychological development. Studies of institution children, since the last war particularly, have had far-reaching effects on the thinking of workers with children and their parents in recent years, though, as early as 1900, Chamberlain was making similar observations of institutionalized children and noting that they were more retarded, apathetic and anxious than children brought up in more normal home environments. Substantial increases in the measured intelligence of retarded orphans were found by Skeels and Dye (1939) when these children were placed in the company of women of very

low intelligence with whom they experienced more emotional interaction than they had formerly known in the orphanage.

More recent studies by Bowlby (1952), Spitz (1945), Spitz and
Wolf (1946), Goldfarb (1943, 1945) and Ribble (1943, 1944) of institutionalized babies and their limited intellectual development as
compared with that of children reared in a warm, reassuring, inter-
active milieu, offer strong confirmation. These studies are relevant to
any study that concerns itself with the growth of intelligence and
intelligent behaviour, and particularly academic attainment. All
emphasize that intelligent behaviour is optimally developed in a
situation where there is acceptance, warmth, constancy, predicta-
bility and flexible free interaction. They confirm that the quality of
the emotional interchange with the significant person or persons in
the child's environment influences the range of cues to which the
child will respond. A rewarding relationship encourages the child to
assimilate and incorporate more experience into his increasingly
elaborated schemata. By contrast, the child who receives no emotional satisfactions is more likely to withdraw into himself. Then
having less social and psychological contact with his environment,
there comes a restriction of awareness to whatever cues might be
available, and inhibition of reaction to situations.

One product of this process is failure to develop potential intelligent behaviour, including that required in intelligence tests and
academic attainment. Vernon (1960) believes that no sharp distinction can be made between intelligence and attainments, and considers that we should not think of intelligence as the main causal factor in attainment. He considers that both are dependent upon or
limited by genetic factors, and states : 'There is no essential difference
between the acquisition of, say, reading skills and the acquisition
of reasoning or other capacities which would normally be regarded
as part of intelligence. Both involve the development of schemata
through exercise with appropriate materials, and their shaping or
correcting by environmental pressures.'

At any intelligence level there is a large amount of variation in
taking advantage of educational opportunity. Four factors in educational motivation have been outlined by de Haan and Havighurst

(1961), each of which is related directly or indirectly to the quality of the emotional and social environment of the child. These are:

1. *Need for achievement* (*nAch*), which is said by McClelland *et al.* (1953) to arise particularly out of mothers training their children to assert their initiative and self-reliance in solving their problems by themselves, while at the same time providing an emotional environment that assures the child of security.

2. *Identification with persons who have gone to college.* A deep unconscious identification with certain adults is formed and the child strives to be like them. These adults are usually 'significant persons' to the child, such as parents, teachers or club leaders. Where one of these has been to college, this often becomes a source of stimulus to academic aspiration.

3. *Social pressure.* In the child's environment there are forces which encourage or discourage him to do well in academic work. These have been the subject of the Davis, Havighurst and Warner hypotheses. The pressure may be exerted by parents, peers, teachers, or the cultural level of the home. If all combine to exert steady pressure in the same direction, the aggregate force can be formidable.

4. *Intrinsic pleasure.* In some people there is a desire to carry on a certain activity for the pleasure it gives, quite independently of whether it is rewarded or approved by any agency outside the person himself. Anne Roe (1953) found this kind of motivation in outstanding experimental physicists whom she studied. They had spent much of their childhood playing with radios and other sorts of equipment.

It is interesting to speculate upon the origins of 4, and tempting to attribute it to some early identification with some person who had such interests. For example, children's activities in painting, music, reading and mechanics are more likely to become permanent when unobtrusively fostered than when the child has to make his own way with no such interest being shown by some identificant. Studies by Shaw and McCuen (1960), Jackson and Marsden (1962) and Smykal (1962) have confirmed separately that the level of attainment a child will reach in school is something that the child brings with him in embryonic form when he enters school.

De Haan and Havighurst (1961) have summarized other studies of
school pupils and college students, and point out the importance of
the emotional inadequacies of under-achievers' environments, their
poorer personal adjustment and their narrower interests compared
with those of achievers. One study they cite at length is that of Haggard (1957), who studied bright high and low achievers in arithmetic.
He found that the high achievers, when compared with low achievers
having the same IQ, 'had by far the best developed and healthiest
egos, both in relation to their own emotions and mental processes
and in their greater maturity in dealing with the outside world of
people and things'. His findings suggested that the high achievers
were more capable in interpersonal relationships and had clear role
concepts. They were more assertive and independent than under-
achievers, and less bound by the constraints of their superiors. If
they felt that undue restrictions were being imposed upon them they
reacted with hostility and self-assertion in order to maintain their
independence and autonomy of thought and action. Haggard concluded that the best way to produce clear thinking (and presumably
higher attainment) is to help children develop into anxiety-free emotionally healthy individuals who are trained to master a variety of
intellectual tasks.

These studies suggest consistently that, for the under-achiever,
something is lacking in the quality of the emotional interaction he
experiences with his significant adults; while, for the high achiever,
there is freedom, acceptance, security, ease and confidence, an atmosphere in which sharing of interests and emotional experiences
promote clarity and freedom of thought and the preconditions for
successful assimilation of stimuli into elaborating inner schemata.

Although the findings are consistent, the literature is not adequate
for the formulation of well based theories. As Floud (1964) has put it:

We still know far too little about the nature of ability and the conditions
of its development. . . . We have no social theory of learning. . . . But
we are still trying to document this process of social-cum-educational
selection and differentiation; we are still trying to enumerate the particular features of life in the different classes which underlie it.

If we are to assume that in order to discover these underlying features of life in the different social classes we need to study family relationships, then a factorial study by Roff (1949) suggests one possible approach. Roff factor analysed the intercorrelations between the thirty scales of the Fels Parent Behaviour Scales to find the main factors. Seven were found adequate to account for the original correlations. These were democratic guidance, concern for the child, permissiveness, parent–child harmony, sociability adjustment of parents, activeness of home, non-readiness of suggestion. Limitations of family relationships under any of these headings, as perceived by the child, might be a source of anxiety or limited intellectual function. Side by side with these are those posited by Stott who listed as sources of anxiety estrangement from parents, desertion threats, inferiority, parental quarrels, precarious relations with parents, and feelings of being discriminated against. In Keller's (1963) statement on the world of the slum child who fails to learn even rudimentary verbal and intellectual skills, she recognized that these children have only a tenuous and spasmodic interaction with adults, and they also have very low self-esteem.

By contrast, Burt (1925) instances his experiences with slum children over forty years ago, which provides a cogent argument against the environmental hypothesis. These children were all suffering severely from some handicap of environment. Nevertheless, they scored highly in tests of intelligence. Of children living in 'very poor' or 'poor' conditions, 28·4 per cent had IQs above 100, 3·1 per cent above 120, and 0·4 per cent above 130. All these children came from homes of deplorably low intellectual status, the majority had received only meagre education, and some had made only half of normal school attendance. Conversely, he knew some children of well-to-do and highly intellectual parents who were 'irremediably dull'. Burt's example seems to imply hidden reasons for such unexpected phenomena. For example it is possible that in spite of the poor material and intellectual conditions in the slum homes, a healthy emotional exchange existed between children and adults; whereas in the homes of well-to-do and highly intellectual parents, the emotional exchange was less conducive to the children's development.

Parent interest is considered by Douglas (1964) to be of crucial importance. He found that children who are encouraged in their studies by their parents do better in each type of test, in picture intelligence tests as well as in those of reading, vocabulary and arithmetic. Children with very interested parents attain higher scores at eight and eleven years in tests of school subjects than they do in picture and non-verbal intelligence tests. At each age, he states, they may be considered as 'over-achievers', and by the same criterion the children of uninterested parents may be considered as 'under-achievers'. He found that in each social class, children have a con-siderable advantage in the eight-year tests if their parents take an interest in their school work, and an even greater advantage at age eleven. He concluded that the influence of parent interest on test performance is greater than that of size of family, standard of home and academic record of the school. Parent interest in school work is, of course, but a manifestation of other forms of interest in the child, logically, because if the parents were not interested in the child partly for his own sake, it would be relatively unlikely for them to be interested in his school work; except, perhaps, in those instances where parents project their own unfulfilled ambitions onto the child in an emotional context that is unfavourable.

Mundy (1957) compared three groups of subjects who had spent an interval of three years between taking two separate Stanford Binet tests in an institution, in a hostel, or under normal life conditions. The differences between IQ increments were significant beyond the one per cent level. This study, together with those of Kagan *et al.* (1961, 1962), confirm the importance of the child–adult relationship. Kagan *et al.* studied changes in intelligence as measured by Binet tests in 140 children between six and ten years old, to whom they also gave Thematic Apperception Tests. Those who gained most in IQ scores showed more themes of curiosity and achievement than those who decreased in IQ. It is probable that these themes and changes in IQ were related to the interaction these children had with their families, since curiosity and the need to achieve are dampened by a constantly thwarting and restrictive situation, but are encouraged in a stimulating one where opportunity is offered and achievement is rewarded. Rosen and d'Andrade (1959) have confirmed this in their study of achievement motivation which they say is fostered by parents setting high goals for their children to attain, by teaching them self-reliance, giving them freedom and autonomy in decision making and encouraging them to take responsibility. If, as Vernon (1960, 1963) posits, there is no sharp distinction between intelligence and attainment, it is probable that the kind of child–adult relationship which encourages achievement motivation and facilitates gains in IQ scores at the same time facilitates attainment.

Some researchers have pointed out that attainment varies with family size and with the ordinal position of the child within the family, suggesting that a child from a large family experiences a different kind of family interaction than one from a small family. Also it seems that an only child or a first child feels a different interaction with his adults than one who has older siblings. Some such hypothesis is necessary if one is to begin to understand the effect of birth rank and family size. Bene (1957) cited a Scottish study in which children having more than three siblings had mean IQ scores of less than 95, while children having no siblings had mean IQ scores of 113, with corresponding gradations in between. Bene confirmed this in her own study by finding that working-class boys from small families pass the grammar school entrance examination more frequently than those from large families, and thought it might be explained by greater ambition in those from the small families. It could equally be that parents of small families are economically better able to support their children through grammar school permitting them to raise their level of aspiration on their children's behalf from an early age; or that parents of small families provide a child–adult relationship which is more conducive to academic aspiration and success.

Other researchers have confirmed the better educational opportunity enjoyed by children of small families. In a study of 687 fifth grade children, Ferreira and Oakes (1960) found a slight inverse relationship (-0.11) between number of siblings and achievement. Douglas (1964) provides much stronger evidence. He discovered that eldest children with one or two siblings do better in secondary selection examinations than would be expected from their measured ability, and later born do worse than their measured ability would indicate. However, only children in his study obtained just the number of places that would be predicted from their ability scores and no more. Douglas suggested that the explanation for this might lie in the stimulus a first born child receives from the presence of a younger sibling. Whether it is friendly or rivalrous or both is an interesting question. Younger children do not seem to experience the same stimulus, and Douglas suggested that they do not suffer so much from comparison as a first child. An extension of Douglas's findings is to be found in a study of the general population by Schachter (1963) who found that a very high proportion of geniuses and famous people are first born or only children. He also found that this group are more likely to become university students, and that their excess increases with each educational level. This pattern of selection has prevailed for the past twenty years. In common with Douglas he thought that some factor other than mere intelligence would be necessary to explain this, but neither made any direct finding with respect to family differences.

Maslow's (1943) classification of needs into a hierarchy of pre-potency is of interest in a discussion of emotional and social variables in relation to attainment. He hypothesized that needs are crucial according to their order of incidence in child development. The most basic are physiological hunger and thirst; next come needs for protection from harm and injury. After these in order come the social needs which are dependent on family relations, needs for affection, esteem and social approval. And finally the need for self-actualization in development of abilities. He suggests that unless the earlier ones are satisfied, the others are likely to be stunted in their development. For example, if social approval and affection are not experienced, self-esteem will not develop properly and this is likely to limit attainment of potential in fields of self-actualization such as intellectual or other achievement.

At this point it is appropriate to go more deeply into the nature of the facilitating interaction of the family. Morrow and Wilson (1961) have commented briefly on the small literature of family relations correlates of student achievement, but report from the extant literature some general findings of a positive relationship with emotionally supportive home conditions which applies alike to elementary school pupils and high school and university students. Parents of high achievers have been found to give their children more praise and approval, to show more interest and understanding, to be closer to their children, to make their children feel more family belongingness and identification with their parents. Under-achievers' parents have been found to be more domineering, to use more severe and frequent punishment, to baby them or push them excessively or hardly at all. Under-achievers' homes tend to have more tension and parental disagreement about standards of behaviour expected of the children. Most of the studies were based on interviews, and although Morrow and Wilson report that many suffered from sampling limitations, they do have some consistency. Elder (1965) confirmed some of these findings in a cross-cultural study in five countries—Mexico, United States, Britain, West Germany and Italy. One thousand people were interviewed and it was found that children who attended secondary school after fifteen years of age came from more permissive homes than those who did not stay on. However, where permissiveness was carried too far, this seemed to have an adverse effect on secondary school attendance. The most successful environment was an equalitarian one in which authority was balanced between parents, and children had some part in decision making.

Child-centredness of the home is an aspect which Kurtz and Swenson (1951) have found to be important. Parents of high achievers have more pride, confidence, affection and interest in their children, read and play with them and identify with their school activities. By contrast, under-achievers have a limited place in the home. The same was found by researchers of the Champaign Community Unit Schools (1961) in their work with gifted children. Over-achievers' parents were more accepting, showed more trust and were more democratic, and the children perceived this. Under-achievers' parents, on the other hand, have been found to have more strongly negative attitudes to their children than do parents of achieving children (Shaw and Dutton, 1962). Himmelweit (1955) found that middle-class children, who usually do better in school than working-class children, felt more accepted, had freer discussion with parents, that they could confide more in them and shared more interests with them. These findings suggest that middle-class children have more child-centred homes.

Overprotectiveness by parents seems also to affect attainment. Hattwick and Stowell (1936), Rickard (1954) and Sutton (1961) made this finding. Under-achievers' parents tended to be over-restrictive and demanding, or to baby their children and expect too little of them. Sutton considered that such domination by overprotection or oversolicitousness may have the effect of retarding the children's ego involvement, aspiration and educational achievement.

Punishment has been described by Davis (1947) as 'one of the most important methods used in United States society to extinguish undesired habits and impel new behaviour', this being one of the motivations of adaptive socialized anxiety. Conversely, rewards are used as stimulation to induce acceptable behaviour. In addition to these two motivators the general question of consistency of control is important; specific forms of control and their consistency or inconsistency are relevant to how a child reacts to school as a learning situation. As Wall (1955) has put it, 'for the child under ten years ... abrupt changes in attitudes and expectations of adults can delay, if not inhibit, his learning, and be destructive of his security and provocative of aggression either turning inward to himself or outward to his environment'. Attitudes and expectations of adults are parallel with and sometimes synonymous with controls. A school child experiences conflict between adults' attitudes and expectations when differences exist between which aspects of the child's behaviour are rewarded or punished at different times and places, for example, at home and at school. Warner, Havighurst and Loeb (1944) have noted how teachers tend to reward middle-class behaviour in the classroom and leave unrewarded, or punish, working-class behaviour. Such a source of conflicting expectations and controls are one possible contributing factor in the poorer adjustment which was found among low achievers by Singer (1961) and Montgomery (1956). The former study showed under-achievers as having feelings of laziness and lack of intellectual ambition, while Montgomery found that high school dropouts felt more hostility towards teachers, police and parents than did their contemporaries who intended staying on at school until graduation, and Morrow and Wilson's under-achieving high school students saw themselves as restless, impulsive and irresponsible.

In other studies defective controls and discipline have been seen to place children at a disadvantage in their adjustment to school and to build up personality problems in other areas of their life space. Severe parental control in early years has been found to stifle the growth of emotional security and the achievement of a confident clear self concept, and also tended to promote feelings of guilt about occasional trial assertions of the ego (Schoeppe, Haggard and Havighurst, 1953), children who are backward in school have been found to have experienced over-strict or weak or vacillating discipline at home (Hora, 1956), under-achieving primary school pupils have experienced severe and frequent though ineffectual punishment (Conklin, 1940), under-achieving high school pupils have known more parental disagreement about standards of behaviour than over-achievers (Tibbetts, 1955), and under-achieving trainee teachers have had domineering parents and sensed more tension at home (Jones, 1955).

While such controls seem to inhibit achievement, other forms of control enhance it. Controls exerted by parents of children with high achievement motivation differ from those used by parents of children with low achievement motivation. The former parents, especially the mothers, punish failure with rejection and reward success with warmth, so that rewards and punishments are emotional in character and therefore dependent upon some closeness of relationship. Rosen and d'Andrade (1959) found that these mothers also tended to be striving and competent and expected their children to be the same. The mothers tended to encourage achievement, while the fathers encouraged independence. Rosen and d'Andrade concluded that superior performance of the high nAch children was more a function of self-reliance and zest in competitive situations, which was encouraged by their parents with this type of control, than it was a function of mere intelligence. Winterbottom (1953) made similar findings. Mothers of children with high achievement motivation differed from mothers of children with low achievement motivation in that they made more demands for evidence of independence and maturity and achievement at early ages, and gave more intense and frequent rewards for fulfilled demands.

Another characteristic of child–adult interaction seeming to facilitate attainment at school is the presence of a democratic atmosphere as defined by justification of policy, joint decision making and willing explanations. Baldwin (1955) claims that democracy is more important than warmth. He found democracy to be the principal factor in promoting gains of up to eight points of IQ in three years. Parents of high achievers are less critical of their children and better able to anticipate their children's responses to questions about themselves. This finding by Peppin (1963) also suggests closer rapport between high achievers and their parents. Morrow and Wilson (1961) found that high achieving boys perceived their families as being more emotionally supportive than underachievers saw their families. High achievers saw their parents as more approving, trusting, affectionate, understanding, encouraging and permissive and providing opportunities for sharing recreation, ideas and confidences.

It is conceivable that a democratic home encourages outgoing forthcoming attitudes of mind and behaviour, while an autocratic one tends to stifle expression. It is also conceivable that forthright and free expression, which is encouraged in a democratic home, also encourages scholastic success, perhaps because there is freer interplay of ideas in the child's thought. Cattell and Sealy (1965) state :

Whereas the correlation of attainment with intelligence appears to remain much the same under different ages and conditions, the connections with personality appear more susceptible to change . . . a socially outgoing child tends to do well at school, whereas at university level the student who is withdrawn . . . does better than the outgoing person, where intelligence is controlled.

Other evidence suggestive of the value of democratic atmosphere and its implied characteristics is provided by Elder (1965), Walsh (1956), Himmelweit (1960) and Wilson *et al.* (1954). Elder's group from democratic families displayed self-confidence, were independent in their judgments and showed ambition. Walsh's low achievers saw themselves as criticized and isolated by their families, restricted in action, and were inadequate in responding to environmental stimuli and unable to express themselves freely and adequately. Himmelweit found that in the families of middle-class adolescents, the high achieving group, authority was more evenly shared than in working-class families. By contrast with the constriction, poor self concepts and inability for self expression in Walsh's sample from undemocratic families, it could be expected conversely that freely interacting families would foster creative intelligence. In a democratic family atmosphere curiosity and flexibility of thought are encouraged and rewarded, while in an autocratic one, curiosity and free thought are dampened and feedback and sharing of ideas is limited.

Guilford (1950) and Wilson, Guilford *et al.* (1954) have posited a complex of abilities that make up creative thinking as follows:

1. *Sensitivity to problems*, which means awareness of defects, deficiencies and needs of the environment.
2. (*a*) *Associative fluency*, the ability to think rapidly of words that meet certain requirements such as synonyms, antonyms.
   (*b*) *Ideational fluency*, or speed in ideation.
3. (*a*) *Spontaneous flexibility*, the ability to strike out in a number of different directions of thought, having regard to reality.
   (*b*) *Adaptive flexibility*, the ability to change one's thinking to suit a changing problem.
4. *Originality*.
5. *Redefinition*, or the ability to improvise.

It is likely that these attributes would develop better in the kind of family where democratic processes are at work, than where autocracy forbids departure from rigidly set limits. In the latter conditions only conformist and convergent thinking are encouraged and creative use of other available cues is inhibited.

Warren and Heist (1960) have reported a relationship between liberal social attitudes and giftedness. They found that gifted college students are less rigid and authoritarian than average students, have wider aesthetic and intellectual interests, and are more creative in their use of ideas. This supports the statement of de Haan and Havighurst (1961) that the person with authoritarian tendencies may depend upon authority persons for his attitudes and is likely to be anxious, rigid and insecure. This kind of anxiety may help him to do well in formal tasks, such as learning grammar and spelling; but he may be unproductive in situations requiring flexible and creative thinking.

Getzells and Jackson (1960, 1962) compared two groups of children : one group averaged 150 in IQ but were below the top 20 per cent in creativity as measured by creativity tests devised by Guilford; the second group were in the top 20 per cent for creativity but averaged only 127 in IQ. The mean IQ for the school was 130. When they were compared on standardized tests of knowledge commonly taught in the schools, both groups were significantly superior to the remainder of the school population. This is interesting because the high creativity low IQ group achieved better in school than average, although they were below average in IQ, suggesting that high creativity promotes high achievement in school, in the sense that children with high creativity scores do better in school than would be predicted from their IQ scores. Less creative children tend more to attain at the level their IQ scores would indicate. There is thus some suggestion that the high creativity group are synonymous with what are variously called plus achievers, high achievers, or achievers. It seems that the creative or 'divergent' pupils are more habituated than the less creative or 'convergent' to make ready use of cues they have received in the past, they can draw on latent ideas more readily and relate them to the test situation, and their incidental learning is greater.

Getzells and Jackson (1962) suggest as an explanation the probability that creativity, which they regard as a cognitive style, is not sampled by ordinary IQ tests. Further, they claim that this additional ability is inextricably linked with general motivational structure. They also hint that modes of child rearing play a part in the growth of creativity. Mothers of highly creative children in their study expressed more dissatisfaction about their own child rearing practices than mothers of the low creativity high IQ group. They were more ready to question their practices and more open-minded, whereas the low creativity high IQ mothers seemed less self-critical in this area, suggesting that the more creative mothers were less rigid in their child rearing, and that they were also less autocratic. The mothers of the high IQs, rather than the mothers of the high creatives, appeared to be more insecure, vigilant about their children's behaviour and choice of friends, and more critical of their children. On the other hand the mothers of the highly creative (who were also the high achievers) worried less about cleanliness, good manners and studiousness, were more interested in their children's 'openness to experience, values, and interests and enthusiasm for life', and more willing to allow divergent individuality and risk taking. The authors maintain that 'the differences between the two groups of children have their source not only in immediate school experiences but in the family environment in which they grow up'.

Developmental tasks

The notion of developmental tasks put forward by Havighurst (1953) is concerned with social development in key areas, four of which have been selected for this study as relevant to school achievement in middle childhood. These are emotional independence, intellectual skills, peer relations and learning an appropriate sex role. The extent to which a child finds success and satisfaction in the achievement of these tasks might be expected to influence his anxiety level, general adjustment and school achievement. Havighurst's definition of a developmental task is 'a task which arises at or about a certain period in the life of the individual, successful achievement of which leads to his happiness and to success in later tasks, while failure leads to unhappiness in the individual, disapproval by the society, and difficulty with later tasks'.

Achieving emotional independence involves developing personal autonomy and the ability to think and act independently of parents and other adults.

The intellectual skills to which Havighurst refers are reading, writing and arithmetic. Acquisition of these fundamental skills constitutes a task necessary for every child to achieve. Since this concept coincides with measures of achievement used in the present study, and it is assumed from the studies of Takano (1959) and others cited earlier in this chapter, that success and satisfaction are in some way related, this task is taken to refer to the child's confidence in achieving these skills and the satisfaction he derives from this.

Peer relationships depend upon the ability of a child to mix with other children of his own age, to make friends and to give and take in social situations. Havighurst considers that the child's chief concern is with this task, and that 'often the key to understanding a child's difficulties with school subjects, or to understanding a discipline problem in class, is given by a knowledge of his difficulties in achieving this particular developmental task'.

Learning an appropriate masculine or feminine social role depends on the identification a child makes with same sexed adults, and the differentiation he makes between the behaviour expected of either sex. The extent to which this role is learned may be gauged by the child's acceptance of his own sex role or whether he is envious of the opposite sex.

The studies selected for review refer in some instances to how far the tasks have been achieved, and in others to the satisfaction the child has found or is finding in these tasks. It is assumed that success and satisfaction go together. The usefulness of the concept of developmental tasks is exemplified in Peck and Havighurst's work (1960) with children who were studied from the age of ten to seventeen years, during which time achievement in these areas of life progressed predictably in spite of the pressures of adolescence which might have been expected to bring about radical changes in developmental trends. The authors state that during these years 'each child tended to show a stable, predictable pattern of character. . . . Each child appeared to maintain very persistently his deeply held feelings and attitudes towards life, and the modes of reacting (to situations) which we call his character structure.' Between ten and thirteen years the overall correlation was 0·78, and between thirteen and sixteen it was 0·92. Peck and Havighurst conclude that 'whatever patterns of moral behaviour and character structure a child shows at ten, he is far more likely than not to display into adolescence and (we believe) for the rest of his life'. De Haan and Havighurst (1961) see failure in developmental tasks as a source of personality and social problems, and posit a class of under-achiever who under-achieves because he is maladjusted and unmotivated as a result of this failure.

Schoeppe, Haggard and Havighurst (1953) studied boys and girls to discover reasons for success or failure in these tasks and their findings show the importance of emotionality and its expression in outlets satisfying to the individual and acceptable to society. They state: 'If a child is to accomplish successfully the developmental tasks required by his society, it is imperative that he master his impulsivity and accept himself so that he can mobilize his energies to deal with social and cultural forces.' They found that the extent to which a child is able to do this depends heavily upon the controls parents use. Children whose parents exerted severe control in the child's formative years were hindered in their development.

There is some discrepancy between the statements of different workers about the relationship of emotional independence to achievement. Rosen and d'Andrade (1959) found that need for achievement (nAch) was fostered by a close involvement of the mothers with their children in which they rewarded success with warmth and punished failure with rejection. Kagan observed further that development of need for achievement thus, surprisingly, seemed most favoured in the context of an emotionally dependent relationship of the child upon the mother, rather than emotional independence. Levy (1933) made similar findings many years earlier. Overprotected children were better in tests of English and vocabulary. He thought the reason for these findings might be that overprotected children live in closer contact with adults and are exposed to more advanced expression than if they mixed more with their peers. It seems likely that these children would find English and vocabulary easier at school. Their skill in these areas would then be rewarded and reinforced by their teachers. The arithmetic performance of Levy's overprotected and dependent children was, by contrast, inferior to that of their peers, suggesting that overprotectiveness does not favour all kinds of achievement.

In other studies emotional dependence has been found to have a retarding effect, which suggests that conversely independence promotes achievement. Morgan and Banker (1938) in a study of fifty-one seventh and eighth grade children reported a negative relationship of −0·80 between persistence in a maze test and parental protectiveness and considered that the overprotected child might be expected to fail more often than the independent child, through inability to persist with a task and to overcome the frustrations experienced in first attempts. More recently, Todd, Terrell and Frank

(1962) in a study of college students relating to differences between normal achievers and under-achievers of superior ability found that male, but not female, under-achievers had significantly greater needs for love and affection than normal achievers. It could be argued also that the students in their study were also less emotionally independent since they had more unsatisfied needs. Erikson (1950b) believes that the growth of personal autonomy is dependent upon the satisfaction of such needs, and Bowlby (1952) has shown how children who are deprived of such satisfactions often display dependent emotional patterns in later life. Warren and Heist (1960) have produced further evidence, consistent with that of Morgan and Banker and of Todd *et al.*, that gifted college students were more independent, confident and mature. Elder (1965) found in a cross cultural study of one thousand in Mexico, United States, Britain, Germany and Italy, that children who went to secondary school after the age of fifteen came from homes where self-reliance and initiative were most encouraged. This suggests that the kind of independence which aids academic achievement in university is needed also in school before the age of fifteen, and probably as early as the junior school years.

Some studies have indicated that achievers characteristically feel confidence in their ability and enjoy intellectual tasks. Todd *et al.* confirmed at a significant level that lower achievers have less confidence that they will do well in academic activities than do norma. achievers, and Warren and Heist stated that gifted students have 'a strong disposition to intellectual activity—a liking for reflective and abstract thought, interest in ideas and conceptualization'. Wall (1955) considered that this confidence and enjoyment should be fostered in young children by ensuring that 'the balance of experience in the child's early years should be on the side of success'; 'the establishment, through success, of the child's confidence in his power to learn, the elimination of the total failures which are so painful and destructive of morale are . . . fundamental contributions to mental health'. Takano's experiment (1959) cited earlier, supports Wall in demonstrating how success experiences increase children's adaptiveness in subsequent problem solving situations, while children who fail initially experience more failure and show less adaptiveness in later tasks. From such experiments it could be hypothesized that initial success encourages confidence and enjoyment in subsequent tasks, and that failure induces a reduction of confidence and enjoyment, leading to further failure.

That favourable attitudes to school, perhaps arising out of success experiences at school, do in fact favourably affect performance is suggested by the findings of Griffiths (1962) who found that even before eleven plus selection results were known to children, attitude scores of successful pupils were almost significantly higher than those of the unsuccessful ones; and that after results were announced, as might be expected, the enthusiasm of the failure group fell faster than that of the success group. Later, in the second year of secondary school, the attitudes to school of C stream grammar school children were superior and more stable than those of the A stream secondary modern group whose enthusiasm had dropped considerably by February of the first year in secondary modern school. These findings suggest that not only do positive attitudes affect performance favourably, but that negative attitudes are reinforced after failure becomes known. After discussing the role of attitudes in achievement, de Haan and Havighurst stated 'the conclusion of various studies is that the gifted person with a high level of achievement has found the way to enjoy himself through educational achievement'. Whether this is so for less gifted high achievers and whether a linear relationship exists between achievement and confidence and enjoyment in intellectual skills and interest in school at this point is an interesting question, and an affirmative answer is indicated.

Peer relationships usually play an increasing role in children's motivations as emotional independence from parents is achieved. It is in middle childhood that they begin to assert their influence. Davis (1947) has stated that 'every adolescent's social behaviour bears the marks of his personal history in relation to his . . . play (peer) group. . . . Cultural behaviour is learned behaviour . . . learned through processes of imitation, identification, competition and cooperation.' If this hypothesis is accepted peer relationships might be expected to affect school performance differently for each social class according to the values that are held by the peer group. If peer relationships are intense and frequent and identification with the group exists, and group values favour school achievement, this could intensify motivation in the child. If the values of the group favour non-intellectual interests, then peer relationships could exert an influence that would lower achievement. Coleman (1959) has pointed out how in many high schools the students' group values are focused upon sports, popular music, dates and cars rather than intellectual activity. Some of these influences are apparent in late middle childhood also, when children are beginning to emulate adolescents. Coleman also stated that high school students are often aware that grades are relative, and in self interest they react negatively to well motivated children who raise the class averages and thus become unpopular. Supporting this, Morrow and Wilson (1961a) found that underachievers saw themselves as belonging to peer groups with negative attitudes to school achievement.[1] A link is here suggested with Schachter's (1963) findings that first born children, who Schachter found in a series of earlier studies to be less popular than other children, form a high proportion of the academically successful scholars although there are no significant differences between the intelligence of first borns and others. Whether their low popularity can be explained by being first born or by their high motivation for academic work with consequent greater isolation, the implication of these studies remains that academic success sometimes goes together with low popularity, and that children and older students who are popular in certain schools tend to be low-achievers.

Robinowitz (1956), however, found for his sample that pupils achieving beyond their level of expectancy were as well accepted by their peers as their fellow pupils in lower achievement categories. He made the further interesting finding, however, that high-achievers felt more doubt and confusion in their peer relationships, but argued that this uneasiness had the effect of making them strive harder for achievement as a means of gaining fuller acceptance in the peer group. Different findings were made by Sandin (1944), Buswell (1953) and the Champaign (Illinois) researchers (1961). Sandin studied 139 non-promoted elementary school children, and found that they were

[1] In passing, there can be little doubt that the structure of a school system can reinforce attitudes and norms of peer groups, in addition to the structure of the relationships within any given type of school or family group.

regarded by their classmates as belonging to a separate group, indicating some lack of acceptance by the main peer group, and the children themselves could perceive this. Buswell found that in elementary schools the highest achievers were the most popular. She considered it possible that a circular process starts when a child is initially unaccepted so that he becomes insecure and then finds it more difficult to succeed; and that high intelligence rather than achievement in itself is what promotes popularity with peers. But her main conclusion was that those who are succeeding in their school work will also be succeeding in their peer relationships. The Champaign studies supported this. Their findings show that high achievers not only were well accepted, but they perceived significantly greater peer acceptance than under-achievers.

Kagan and Moss (1962) have stated that 'the relevance of sex role identification in directing behavioural choices is supported by investigations indicating that the child begins to differentiate the culture's definition of masculine and feminine characteristics and activities very early in development'. They comment on the work of Hartup and Zook (1960) who reported that even three-year-old children are aware of the interests and objects that comprise the exterior decor of males and females in American culture. They found rapid sex role differentiation in children from three to four years of age. Kagan and Moss also instanced several of Kagan's own studies and those of some of their colleagues of the Fels Research Institute, Ohio, which indicate that 'children from five to ten years of age view the male, in relation to the female, as more aggressive, dominant, punitive, more fear arousing, and less friendly and nurturant'. The authors stated that 'the most dramatic and consistent finding of their study was that many of the behaviours exhibited by the child during the period six to ten years of age, and a few between three to six years, were moderately good predictors of theoretically related behaviours during early adulthood'. Sex typed activity was one of the most stable areas of behaviour from the age of six to ten years, and showed a high degree of continuity for males and females from early school years to adulthood.

They continue by stating that the masculine and feminine quality of an activity or an object is apparently one of the first questions implicitly asked by the child. Having determined the answer to this question, his behaviour towards it (i.e. approach or avoidance) will depend upon his sex role identification. If this is so, then it would seem to follow that children who see educational attainment as conflicting with their sex role identification will be less motivated to achieve educationally than those who perceive it to be consonant. Class differences regarding the roles of male and female would probably have some influence on whether children would perceive conflict or consonance. The authors conclude that 'the universe of appropriate behaviours for males and females is delineated early in development; and it is difficult for the child to cross these culturally given frontiers without considerable conflict and tension'. This statement suggests some relevance of sex role identification to education, in particular where academic and cultural striving is considered effeminate, as perhaps in some working-class subcultures (Davis 1948). It suggests that the child who has not learned an appropriate sex role will be subjected to social situations which are likely to provoke anxiety and help to bring about a decrement or an increment in educational attainment, depending on the subculture from which the child originates.

Since sex role identification would appear to have some relevance to education it is surprising that, although the concept has been recognized by many workers, the literature is void of any studies concerning the relationship between the two.

Summary

Social class studies have been traced from Burt's (1937) exploration of social class factors in school backwardness, in which he assessed the importance of poverty, population density, family size, poor health and inadequate general knowledge, to more modern studies in which consistent findings have been made that middle-class children still achieve more highly than working-class children in spite of the amelioration of some of the grosser aspects of environment to which Burt referred.

Factors receiving attention since Burt's early work have been, for example, methods of control and child rearing (Davis, 1944, 1947,

1948); cultural values (Campbell, 1951); family abnormalities, cultural, material and motivational factors (Fraser, 1955); and differences between linguistic development and verbal communication styles in working-class and middle-class homes (Bernstein, 1960, Riessman, 1962, Keller, 1963). Douglas (1964) has demonstrated ways in which schools react to children's social class characteristics in such a way as to widen the gap that originally existed between children's chances of future academic development. Anxiety studies were reviewed next and reference was made to the mixed and contradictory findings. From laboratory studies it was concluded that simple reflex learning tends to be facilitated by anxiety which is in some way related to eagerness in mental set; but anxiety was seen to be an inhibitor of more complex learning.

In school learning, findings become less clearcut, even contradictory and confused. The Davis hypothesis that adaptive socialized anxiety promotes achievement in middle-class children, and the generalization of Lynn (1955) that high achievers who tend to come from middle-class families are the more anxious, were tested by Hallworth (1961), but he found that secondary modern school children, not the highest achievers in primary school, were the more anxious.

This is illustrative of many inconsistencies in the research in anxiety and achievement. The possibility was considered that differing degrees of anxiety affect performance in different tasks in different ways, and that individual differences in the foci of anxiety would also be of some importance in the relationship between anxiety and performance. It was particularly noted that there is no coherent theory of the role of anxiety in relation to academic achievement.

Studies of child–adult relationships and developmental tasks in relation to school performance were also reviewed, and the literature was found to be less extensive, particularly on the question of how these relate to social class as a correlate of attainment. Himmelweit (1960), Morrow and Wilson (1961) and Floud (1964) expressed this. Much earlier Binet (1909) emphasized that social forces surrounding the child were important for the development of ability and attainment. It is thus strange that sixty years later a clear theory of social interaction and its relation to learning has not yet been delineated. However, of the authors reviewed, Piaget (1947) and Hebb (1949), Bowlby (1952), Ribble (1943, 1944), Spitz (1945), Spitz and Wolf (1946), and Goldfarb (1943, 1945), who are representative, have at least agreed that social and emotional interaction between children and significant adults enhances or limits the growth of intelligent behaviour. There is thus agreement between the findings of researchers in several countries.

Work on developmental tasks has been mostly confined to the studies of Havighurst and his associates, though overprotectiveness which bears some apparent inverse relationship to emotional independence, one of the developmental tasks, has been researched by Morgan and Banker (1938) as has self reliance and initiative (Elder, 1965) and independence, confidence and maturity (Warren and Heist, 1960).

Sex role taking and peer relations are examples of other developmental tasks which Havighurst posited were necessary to achieve for general personality development. Kagan and Moss (1962) considered that the masculine or feminine quality of an activity or an object is one of the first questions implicitly asked by the child. Having determined the answer to this question, his behaviour towards it, whether approach or avoidance, will depend on his sex role identification.

Studies of peer group relations related to achievement were generally in agreement that children who were achieving well, tended also to be doing well in their peer relationships, but this needs to be interpreted in relation to the social class of the peer groups, whose attitudes to school attainment might vary. Peer groups could thus have differential effects on the individual child's school performance, according to the attitudes and aspirations held by the group.

There has been no attempt in this chapter to make a sharp distinction between British and American research. They are in quite remarkable agreement with each other, except in the work on anxiety, and this, it appears, is due largely to the confusion which exists in defining anxiety.

Part 2

The empirical study

3

Aims and methods

Aims of the research were to discover aspects of the social and personal adjustment of children which are most associated with academic success and failure; to make some contribution to our understanding of the links between social class and academic achievement; and to clarify further the association which exists between anxiety and achievement.

Such an aim is comprehensive, and rightly involves enquiring into every aspect of a child's life. To bring it into manageable proportions, following an extensive review of previous research in achievement in Chapter 2, areas of children's interaction with their environment were selected which from the literature seemed to be most relevant to the research problem.

From the hypotheses and findings of the researches of the Fels Institute and others (Baldwin *et al.*, 1949) a considerable number of areas of importance in children's personality development were identified. It was assumed in the planning of the study that these areas might have a critical influence upon children's intellectual development and educability.

Other variables which are known from the literature to have some association with learning behaviour also included in the study are age, sex, family size, and number of schools attended, and of course social class itself.

An anxiety measure was also included because of the conflicting reports about its relation to learning ability and because it forms a central ingredient of the child's adjustment to his environment.

In most studies, anxiety has been regarded as a non-specific condition, rather than as something with a specific focus peculiar to the individual and his situation. While it can be agreed that generalizations can be made about anxiety, perhaps not enough interest has been taken in aspects of anxiety that are, to some extent, unique to the individual. It is possible that the confusion present in the literature of anxiety is to some extent due to this non-specific view of anxiety. Anxiety is seen in this study in terms of the kinds of things children generally worry about, and some attention is paid to specific life areas that represent the main foci of anxiety in children, e.g. worry about growing up, school performance, peer relations and parents. It is possible that children's behaviour is affected not only by pervasive anxiety but also, and perhaps more directly, by concern felt in one or more of these specific life areas. It was possible that some of the ambiguity, or ambivalence as Reed calls it, for which anxiety research is notorious might be resolved by studying each of these areas individually. The anxiety inventory used in the study was previously used in studies by Himmelweit and is shown in Appendix 5.[1]

For the areas of family and child–adult relations, variables were drawn from those investigated by the Fels Research Institute, Ohio, where longitudinal studies of parent–child interaction have been conducted over several decades. Their conceptual framework has been built from a global view of parent behaviour. From their framework those variables were chosen which were considered to be of greatest relevance to educational achievement, and which could be included most effectively and usefully in a study such as the present one. The Fels Parent Behaviour Rating Scales are built around thirty variables, which were originally posited by Champney (1941). The scales were intended to be used in home interview schedules as an outline for the assessment of observed interaction between the parent and the child. However in the present study a large sample was available drawn from a number of schools and it was preferred to secure some assessment of the children's own perceptions of their home relationships rather than to attempt any objective assessment as an observer from outside. This was done in the belief that the children's perceptions are of greater moment than assessments by an outsider, however valid, objective, and reliable they might be.

The variables considered in forming the questionnaire for the area

[1] I am obliged to Professor Himmelweit for suggesting the use of the inventory in this research.

of family and child–adult interactions were demonstrativeness, rapport, child-centredness, sharing of interests and hobbies, frequency of contact, understanding, hostility, over-protectiveness, democracy, controls and discipline, parental discord and sibling rivalry.

The concept of developmental tasks, put forward by Havighurst (1953) was a further source of suitable variables. Peer relationships, emotional independence, learning an appropriate sex role, and confidence and enjoyment in intellectual skills are areas which seemed crucial to a child's development, and which might affect school attainment.

An attempt was made also to consider the importance of certain aspects of father–child and mother–child relationships. Consonance between the values of home and school, and adjustment to school and teachers are thought by Wall (1962) to have some influence upon school achievement and were therefore included.

The sample

The choice of a primary school sample was dictated by numerous considerations, the more important of which are as follows:

1. Wastage of talent begins in the primary schools, if not before. This has been confirmed in the literature reviewed.
2. Children of all levels of ability and attainment are present in primary schools.
3. It is the last opportunity to study children before the differential effects of divergent types of secondary school start to occur, and before the effects of mixing with more homogeneous peer groups begin to manifest themselves in the setting of aspirational levels and academic and vocational interests.
4. Results of recently taken selection tests were available for use as achievement measures.
5. Probably most important of all was that in this year of education, differences between high and low achievers rapidly increase. Shaw and McCuen (1960) made this finding after studying children at all grade levels. By choosing children of this age it was thus

73

possible to make the most distinct comparisons between high and low-achievers.

The schools

The schools from which the sample was derived were in two different boroughs of Middlesex, now part of the Greater London Council. These two areas differ in many ways. One, west of London, has a long history as a middle-class dormitory suburb. Its middle-class character is largely intact except for certain areas which contain a little light industry. The other area, to the north of London, contains a diversified industrial area. It has a history of heavy industry extending back 150 years, with recent additions of light industry. While this borough also contains a large middle-class district, the schools were selected from those in or near the industrial area. The choice of these two areas afforded an excellent opportunity to include in the sample a full range of socio-economic class representation.

The children and the schools

The aim was to explore factors which affect children of all social classes and intelligence levels, and of both sexes. Therefore the entire population of the top primary classes of ten schools in two contrasting suburbs was included in the investigation. The sample consisted of 489 children. At one extreme was a school where 76 per cent of the fathers were manual working class. At the other was a school where 84 per cent of the fathers did non-manual work. Boys and girls were about evenly represented. IQ distribution extended over the whole primary school range of between less than 80 to 140+ yielding a mean of 107 and standard deviation of 13.

Social class

Occupational class of fathers was discovered by use of two questions: (a) 'What is the name of your father's job?' (b) 'Carefully describe the sort of work he does.' The mere naming of a father's occupation by a child usually produces ambiguous, misleading and useless information. By using the second item, there is a considerable gain in clarification of the precise nature of the occupation. For example, in answer to the first question, two children might answer 'engineer', while in answer to the second, the first child might state 'he works a lathe', and the second child 'he designs bridges'. The former would be in class 6, whereas the latter would be in class 1. Himmelweit reported that junior school children are able to describe their fathers' occupation accurately enough and in sufficient detail for valid classifications of occupational class to be made. In the present research this was confirmed. The correlations of 0·29 and 0·35, usual in the literature, is further evidence of the validity of this procedure.

The answers were coded according to the Hall-Jones Prestige Scale of Occupations, with slight modification of the scale as in previous studies of the London School of Economics. The occupational coding scale was as follows:

Hall-Jones category rank	Description of occupation	Rank in Himmelweit modified scale
1	Professional and high administrative	1
2	Managerial and executive	2
3	Inspectional, supervisory and other non-manual (higher grade)	3
4	a. Routine white collar	4
	b. Foreman	5
5	Skilled manual	(5) 6
6	Semiskilled manual	(6) 7
7	Unskilled	(7) 8

The schools and social class

Tables 3·1, 3·2 and 3·3 show the social class distribution by school. It can be seen that the children represented all occupational classes, and the schools themselves varied in their social class structure. On the one hand, three schools were predominantly manual working class, four schools were predominantly middle class non-manual, and the remaining three were almost evenly manual and non-manual. It will be seen from these tables that all of the social classes were well represented, and moreover, class composition within the schools was varied enough to justify the claim that the schools were a good representation of the varying social class structures of the different suburbs in which schools, generally, are located.

Table 3.1

The number of children of eight social classes (father's occupation) at each school

	Father's occupational category								
	Manual				Non-manual				
	8	7	6	5	4	3	2	1	
School	VII	VI	V	IVb	IVa	III	II	I	Total
0	5	13	18	3	4	3	—	1	47
1	2	12	31	13	3	13	5	1	80
2	1	7	29	6	4	8	3	5	63
3	2	6	15	1	3	5	6	—	38
4	3	3	13	3	12	14	7	3	58
5	2	6	13	2	4	7	10	2	46
6	1	5	19	3	8	4	3	5	48
7	—	5	9	8	11	5	4	3	45
8	—	1	3	11	4	2	2	—	23
9	—	—	6	6	2	16	5	6	41
Total	16	58	156	56	55	77	45	26	489

Social class and verbal ability

Tables 3.2 and 3.3 show the relationship between IQ and social class in our sample as a whole. The potential university group (126 +) is weighted heavily (two-thirds) in favour of those children whose fathers were engaged in white collar jobs.

Although the high average and grammar school groups (106–125) were almost evenly weighted between all social class levels, in the lower levels of verbal ability the proportions were reversed, i.e. of those with ratings of less than 106, 73 per cent had manual working-class fathers. A clear inverse relationship between social class and measured ability is thus once more confirmed.

Table 3.2

Distribution of sample by verbal ability and social class

Verbal IQ	Social class								Total
	8 VII	7 VI	6 V(b)	5 V(a)	4 IV	3 III	2 II	1 I	
University 126–135+	—	2	14	5	5	16	14	8	64
G.S. 116–125	6	6	29 (112)	15	10	18 (104)	15	9	108
High average Not G.S. 106–115	4	14	25	13	16	21	9	6	108
Average 96–105	5	26	50 (153)	13	16 (56)	10	5	2	127
Dull to average <96	1	10	38	10	8	12	2	1	82
Totals	16	58	156	56	55	77	45	26	489

Table 3.3 in which social class has been collapsed into manual and non-manual groupings, yields a Chi^2 value of 38.2; $p = < .001$.

Overall the trend suggests that the tests of verbal ability are biased in favour of middle-class children, or that the working-class milieu militates against the development of verbal ability. The relationship between measured intelligence and social class is, of course, very

Table 3.3

Distribution of the sample by verbal ability and social class, collapsed into manual and non-manual categories

		Social class		
		8 7 6 5	4 3 2 1 Managerial and white-collar	
Verbal IQ		*Manual*	*clerical*	*Total*
University	126+	21 ⎫ 77	43 ⎫ 95	64
G.S.	116–125	56 ⎭	52 ⎭	108
High average Not G.S.	106–115	56 ⎫	52 ⎫	108
Average	96–105	94 ⎬ 153 ⎫ 209	33 ⎬ 56 ⎫ 118	127
Dull to average	<96	59 ⎭	23 ⎭	82
Totals		286	203	489

Chi² was computed using the above 10 cell table, yielding Chi² value of 38·2, p = <·001, highly significant, confirming numerous studies of social class reviewed in chapter 2.

well established in studies in both the United States and Britain, as is discussed in Chapter 2.

The criterion of academic achievement

Objective tests of academic ability and attainment which have been in almost universal use throughout Britain since the Education Act of 1944 were used as the criterion of achievement. All children in primary schools were required to take these tests, and the results were used as the principal criterion upon which children were selected for grammar (academic) school or other forms of secondary education. Although there is currently much criticism of these tests, most valid objection to them is the use to which they have been put, namely selection at eleven-plus, which it was the Labour Government's policy to abolish in favour of comprehensive education with no selection. This policy is being continued by most Local Education Authorities in Britain.

The desirability of using these or any other tests as predictors at the age of eleven is open to very serious doubt on social and educational grounds. However, for assessing academic attainment they are extremely valuable and they are unequalled in Britain as objective, reliable and valid tests, being the product of national research over more than twenty years. There is a high correlation between all three tests: verbal ability, English and arithmetic. For the sample used in this study, correlations were

	Verbal	*English*
English	0·903	—
Arithmetic	0·849	0·921

As can be seen, the correlations were so high as to justify aggregating the scores on all three and treating the result as an overall assessment of attainment as has been customary in allocating children to secondary schools.[1]

The questionnaire method

In planning a study the interview method may seem the most attractive because it offers opportunity of obtaining rich data reflecting the individuality of each of the subjects in a more vivid and personal way than could be expected from the use of questionnaires. While recognizing the merits of the interview as a research method, it was decided not to use it but to proceed with the questionnaire method for several reasons. It would have been impractical and less efficient in the present study to interview so many pupils in schools because

[1] Eleven-plus tests have been produced in the last two decades by the National Foundation for Educational Research in England and Wales, and Moray House in Scotland, and are comparable.

of the time involved, the need to preserve some degree of anonymity, the personal nature of the enquiries and the question of the diversity of the data sought. An immediately compelling reason was that the field work had to be completed within a brief period of four weeks in the final school term between the examinations and the end of the school year.

Other reasons for using the questionnaire method were as follows:

By using questionnaires a large number of children could be included, affording adequate numbers upon which to base conclusions. If any valid generalizations were to be made, a large sample was essential.

Access to schools is not always easy to arrange, so the method used enabled the maximum use to be made of the limited time which county education officers and headmasters could reasonably allow for a researcher to be in the schools.

The method permitted a good measure of objectivity in assessing and coding the responses of the subjects. It enabled all the children to react to identical stimuli and to record their own perceptions of their social relationships at their own pace in a simple way. The children might have felt a little freer to give frank responses because the method is less personal than interviewing.

During the initial framing of items for use in the questionnaire discussions were held with people having a background in psychology, child development, sociology and primary school teaching, as to the best ways of measuring the variables that were to be included in the study.

The items for each variable were framed and selected on the criteria of their intelligibility to the whole range of children in top primary classes, their neutral tone in not being likely to offend or arouse annoyance or resentment, and their potential for stimulating the interest and cooperation of the children. They were then used in pilot studies. Some items were framed so as to ask about grownups rather than parents, where a direct personal question about parents might have caused resistance.

Furthermore, the study was not concerned so much with parents as with children's relationships with their most significant adults. The children were instructed therefore to think of 'the most important grown-ups in their lives' when giving their responses, in order to allow for those homes which contained other adults in addition to, or as substitute for, parents.

Besides the question of tact and the need to include all significant adults, the items had to be simple to enable children of all intellectual levels to comprehend. Since all children in the top primary class of each school were included in the study, the items had so far as possible to be comprehensible to children in the lower bands of intelligence, while not seeming too childish to those in the higher band.

The groups of items were not expected to constitute scales, but rather to be indices of broad areas of behaviour. In terms of the definitions which have been given, they were thought to be appropriate and, therefore, to have face validity. Although face validity lacks value, it was expected that data from items so arranged would be at least as reliable and valid as data from interviews. Cattell (1965) states that the highest reliability between ratings given by different interviewers is in the region of $+0.3$ and $+0.4$. In the event, eight of the eleven *a priori* areas were found to have this level of reliability, using the split half method with the Spearman-Brown correction.

Emphasis was given to breadth of coverage rather than to the design of precise scales in one or two areas. A broad approach to the problem was thought to be appropriate for the reason that the research literature had not indicated which areas were of the greatest importance in children's learning ability and educational development.

The object was to chart some of the most significant areas, after which it would then be appropriate to devise precise scales that would accurately measure these areas. Having devised the questionnaire, so as to elicit as wide a sampling of data as possible, the resultant data were well suited to factor analysis by which method factors or what might be called 'syndromes' are extracted which are based on the matrix of correlations between the items.[1]

[1] Factor analysis cannot be described satisfactorily in very simple terms. It is a very complex mathematical process. Before computers arrived, it would have taken perhaps a dozen people some months to process the present data. Yet, roughly speaking, it is similar to what we all do every day of our lives

Pilot studies

To test the questionnaire items four pilot studies were conducted with 120 children in two different schools which were representative of primary schools in general. One was in a middle-class suburb, and the other in a working-class suburb. Pupils of all streams took part as it was intended that all should be included in the main study. This selection ensured that the full range of ability was represented and could be considered in the selection of the most suitable items from the pilot questionnaires. The pilot studies were conducted to test the meaningfulness of the items to children of eleven years, to discover which items produced a sufficiently satisfactory spread of response to be included in the final questionnaire, to gauge how many items children could answer in the time which was to be allowed for their actual administration in the study proper, and to evolve the best methods of administering them.

To discover if items were meaningful to the children, the questionnaires were submitted for their comments and queries. The children were then told that nobody else would see the way they answered, and it was made clear that the study was of no concern to the school. This was considered necessary in order to ensure that the children felt free to state frankly what they thought rather than something to please or avoid trouble with the teacher.

For a few children some items were more difficult to understand than had been anticipated when they were initially framed, and were rephrased for the next pilot study in a clearer form while retaining their essential meaning.

---

when we process information and, by reflection, turn it into a new idea, concept or schema. Eysenck (1953) likens it to what a doctor does when he diagnoses a disease or a syndrome from data coming to him from the patient, whether this is a visible symptom, a verbal account of feelings or whatever. The data are processed (fitted together logically) and a factor (syndrome or disease, etc.) is abstracted.

Similarly, a scientist may pronounce a new law or theory by processing a large body of data in this manner and arranging it into a new schema which takes into account all relevant knowledge to hand, thus synthesizing a new concept, theory or law. Factor analysis does this, using statistical correlation as the foundation.

During the pilot studies it was soon discovered that children of all intelligence levels were capable of responding to quite a large number of easily understood items. Fears that they would lose interest or panic at the sight of what appeared to be a formidable set of questionnaires proved to be groundless. What did emerge was that their confidence could be gained easily and doubts about their ability to complete the questionnaires could be eliminated by careful presentation with clear reassuring instructions.

Distributions of the responses showed the discriminatory power of each item. There was a wide range in the patterning of the responses. Some items came fairly close to 50 per cent responses either way and these were retained. Others produced responses all tending in the one direction. These items were obviously useless and were discarded altogether to be replaced by others, or emphasis of meaning was altered in one direction or the other in order to evoke a better spread of response.

At every stage the practice was to be alone with the class in each session. The purpose of this was to give the children maximum confidence that their responses were to be known only to the researcher. Teachers were cooperative about this, and it can be confidently claimed that the children generally reacted to the items with the greatest possible frankness. Children of ten or eleven years are usually helpful and cooperative with strangers, and most were pleased to have a new task to do that gave them a rest from the more usual classroom work.

The 'worries' inventory

The 'worries' inventory was used earlier by Himmelweit in a study of middle- and working-class adolescents and by Bruckman (1964) in her study of need for achievement. It is very suitable for use in the classroom situation with children of junior school age and all levels of ability, because the items are easy for young children to understand, all relating to matters which concern children, and the inventory can be completed in ten minutes by most children of about ten years of age. A split half reliability test yielded a reliability coefficient of 0·88 for this inventory.

4

Results and discussion

The analysis of the research data will be discussed under the following headings: background variables (including social class, sex, age, number of schools attended, family size); then the factors,[1] and lastly, anxiety. Straight correlations, then multiple and partial correlations will be discussed in relation to achievement and social class.

Background variables

Social class

Social class with its customary correlation of $+0.30$ to $+0.35$ is long established and was confirmed in this study. Since the relevance of this is discussed in other parts of this book, no further discussion follows at this point.

Sex

Sex differences in children's motivation and attitudes related to achievement were suspected to exist and the results were analysed for each sex separately.[2] Table numbers 4·1, 4·2 and 4·3 show the differences between boys and girls. For girls there were some factors which had a greater association with academic performance than

---

[1] Appendices 1, 2, 3 and 4 describe the procedures used. The factors are set out in Appendix 4, which contains the items to which the children responded and the extent to which each of these items contributed to each individual factor.

[2] The practice of analysing separately for boys and girls is based on an assumption that the two sexes may show quite different relationships between achievement and personality or background variables. This was in fact shown to be true. See also Eysenck and Cookson (1969) and Entwistle and Cunningham (1968).

for boys, while for boys other factors were of greater importance. As the tables show for girls the factors of greater importance than for boys were factors 3, 4, 8, 10, 12 and 26 which can be studied in detail in Appendix 2. It helped girls, more than boys apparently if parents

Table 4.1

Correlations of background variables, achievement and social class

	Achievement		Social class	
Variable	*Boys*	*Girls*	*Boys*	*Girls*
Social class	$35\S$	$29\ddagger$	—	—
Age	07^{ns}	-06^{ns}	-11^{ns}	-01^{ns}
Family size	$-13^{\star}$	$-21\ddagger$	$-16\dagger$	-11^{ns}
Number of schools	-05^{ns}	-05^{ns}	00^{ns}	04^{ns}

$\star = p < \cdot 05$ ns = not significant
$\dagger = p < \cdot 01$ $\S = p < \cdot 0001$
$\ddagger = p < \cdot 001$

were non-indulgent yet shared interests with them, if their thinking was not dominated by parents and if there happened to be a strongly intellectual and enterprising spirit in the family. Academically successful girls could afford to be of a less striving nature than boys, and they made less distinction than unsuccessful girls between the sex roles of boys and girls. (For factor tables, see Appendix 2.)

For boys, factors 1, 20, 24, 25, 31, 32, were more closely associated with achievement. Boys' achievement, compared with that of girls, appeared from the analysis to be more dependent on academic aspiration and parental support, non-protectiveness on the part of the parents, the consonance of values between home and school, the absence of a strong need for closeness to parents, a feeling of independence of action, a sense of sibling rivalry combined with accessibility of parents and feelings of confidence in their own intellectual skills.

However, the differences between the sexes were not so impressive as the similarities. In effect, the factors which seemed to promote achievement in boys held for girls also, and the sex differences can be largely disregarded. The factors are discussed at greater length presently.

Age

Jinks (1964) found that younger children are disproportionately assigned to lower streams. It was hypothesized in this study that, similarly, younger children would be at a disadvantage in objective tests of ability and attainment, in spite of the adjustments for age which are made in such tests as a matter of routine.

It is reassuring to find that the tests do in fact make proper allowance for age difference. The hypothesis was therefore rejected. That result was of course to be expected. It would be going too far to say that it was unnecessary to include this in the study, but in the event it is useful and gratifying to note that tests are in fact more objective and reliable than the opinions some teachers have of their pupils, opinions that lead them to place children in streams, unwittingly, on the basis of age. This should act as a warning to the great number of people who favour the abolition of testing in favour of teachers' assessments. There is a serious danger that by abolishing testing, even though it is true that the tests discriminate in favour of middle-class children, greater injustice may be done to able children who do not satisfy the subjective criteria of the teachers who allocate them to their future places in education. This kind of injustice may well result from bias attributable to age as well as that arising out of social class differences between children.

Number of schools attended

The disruption involved in changing schools can be expected to have disastrous effects for some children. The extent of the effects will depend on the sensitivity of the individual child, the moral support he receives when changing schools, his ability to become accepted by his new peers, the degree of continuity or discontinuity in his studies which results from the changes, and his capacity for relating to new teachers. It may be that changes of school will add to some children's flexibility in making new relationships and in adapting to new learning situations.

In the present study the effect of changing schools appeared to be very small; a correlation of -0.05 for both sexes was obtained. However, of the 489 children in the sample, it must be stressed that only 14 per cent had attended more than two schools, and the average achievement score for the children was hardly any different from the general sample averaging 107 points on the aggregated scores of Verbal, English and Arithmetic tests.

The small amount of difference between children who have attended few or many schools as indicated by the correlation of -0.05 is reassuring, but it would be dangerous to conclude that changing schools has no appreciable effect on any individual child. It can be critical for a sensitive child and the lack of continuity in social relationships may have more serious effects on future social adjustments than upon educational development.

Family size

According to Douglas (1964) a child of any ability from a large family had a 50 per cent greater chance of finding himself in a low stream, and for any social class level a similar greater chance of not being selected for grammar school. Since family sizes tend to be greater among working-class people, there can be little doubt that family size contaminates the social class variable.

In analysing the present data, when social class was partialled out, the correlations between family size and achievement were reduced, though not markedly (see partial correlations, Table 4·2).

Apart from social class of all the background variables examined, family size has the greatest association with achievement, correlation of -0.13 (p $<$ ·05) for boys, and -0.21 (p $<$ ·001) for girls. Douglas's findings are here again confirmed. Douglas explained how family size militates against educational development. He suggested that poorer material care, poorer physical home surroundings and poorer nutrition arising out of the need to economize, and poorer management of the home may be responsible in some large families for the tendency of children from those families not to achieve as well as other children. He found that children from families of six or more children were at a distinct disadvantage in education compared with those from smaller families—even when their fathers were in the professional and managerial groups of occupations, which one might have supposed would cancel out the influence of family size. In fact it did no such thing.

For other explanations and for fuller treatment of this topic the reader is referred to Douglas (1964).

The factors, achievement and social class

The data of the investigation were intended to be diverse, and consequently a large number of factors was expected to emerge from the factor analysis. No less than twenty-five primary factors were derived with factor variances higher than 1·0, which is the Guttman criterion. In addition to the twenty-five primary factors, seven second order factors and two third order factors were computed. Nearly all of the factors are capable of theoretical interpretation. However, particular attention is given in this section only to those factors which account for most of the variance in the criterion of academic achievement, namely the aggregated scores on Verbal, English and Arithmetic tests which were once used for selecting and allocating pupils to secondary schools.

Partial correlations

One of the more general aims of the study was to try to establish the precise role of social class in the academic development of school children up to the age of eleven. The well-established relationship between social class and academic achievement, with correlations of the order of 0·30 to 0·35 being common in the literature still requires a great deal more explanation than has yet been found. The social class variable was therefore partialled out in order to see if the correlations of any factors with the criterion would be enhanced or lessened. That is to say, social class was held constant. If social class were of any great account we would expect by partialling it out to find that some of the correlations would diminish markedly if not be eliminated altogether, while other factors would remain as key variables independent of social class.

Table 4·2 compares the correlations of the factors with achievement when social class is included and when it is partialled out. It can be seen that partialling out social class made only marginal differences to the correlations—so small that we could conclude that social class as an independent variable is of little account. This is an unexpected finding, since a few of the factors were significantly associated with social class at the ·01 per cent level. Also, the sample included the whole spectrum of social class and this would have maximized the influence of social class in our calculations.

The partial correlations demonstrate that the associations which have been found to exist between the factors and educational achievement are relatively independent of social class.

Table 4.2

Correlations and partial correlations of factors with the achievement criterion

Factor number	Original product-moment correlation		Partialling out social class		Correlation of factor with social class	
	Boys	Girls	Boys	Girls	Boys	Girls
1	$45^{\S}$	$30^{\S}$	$39^{\S}$	$28^{\ddagger}$	$26^{\ddagger}$	$14^{\star}$
2	$-22^{\ddagger}$	$-27^{\ddagger}$	$-18^{\dagger}$	$-24^{\ddagger}$	$-15^{\star}$	$-16^{\dagger}$
3	$14^{\star}$	$32^{\S}$	12^{ns}	$30^{\S}$	08^{ns}	11^{ns}
4	$-14^{\star}$	$-36^{\S}$	$-14^{\star}$	$-33^{\S}$	-03^{ns}	$-18^{\dagger}$
5	$20^{\dagger}$	$16^{\dagger}$	$18^{\dagger}$	$15^{\star}$	08^{ns}	07^{ns}
6	-09^{ns}	-09^{ns}	-11^{ns}	-09^{ns}	05^{ns}	-02^{ns}
7	$-17^{\dagger}$	$-23^{\ddagger}$	$-17^{\dagger}$	$-23^{\ddagger}$	-05^{ns}	-02^{ns}
8	-09^{ns}	$-23^{\ddagger}$	-06^{ns}	$-22^{\ddagger}$	-09^{ns}	-08^{ns}
9	$-21^{\ddagger}$	$-20^{\dagger}$	$-24^{\ddagger}$	$-16^{\dagger}$	05^{ns}	$-18^{\dagger}$
10	$34^{\S}$	$45^{\S}$	$28^{\ddagger}$	$41^{\S}$	$23^{\ddagger}$	$26^{\ddagger}$
11	-03^{ns}	08^{ns}	00^{ns}	06^{ns}	-06^{ns}	05^{ns}
12	-09^{ns}	$-21^{\ddagger}$	$-15^{\star}$	$-19^{\dagger}$	$12^{\star}$	$-13^{\star}$
13	-07^{ns}	$-12^{\star}$	-09^{ns}	-11^{ns}	05^{ns}	-05^{ns}
14	-02^{ns}	05^{ns}	-02^{ns}	04^{ns}	00^{ns}	03^{ns}
15	00^{ns}	00^{ns}	02^{ns}	00^{ns}	-04^{ns}	00^{ns}
16	$-18^{\dagger}$	$-14^{\star}$	$-15^{\star}$	$-13^{\star}$	$-13^{\star}$	-07^{ns}

Factor number	Original product-moment correlation		Partialling out social class		Correlation of factor with social class	
	Boys	*Girls*	*Boys*	*Girls*	*Boys*	*Girls*
17	09^{ns}	19†	07^{ns}	18†	05^{ns}	07^{ns}
18	10^{ns}	14★	05^{ns}	15★	17†	—01^{ns}
19	—21‡	—21‡	—23‡	—20†	00^{ns}	—10^{ns}
20	22‡	12★	20†	09^{ns}	09^{ns}	11^{ns}
21	—22‡	—17†	—19†	—14★	—12★	—11^{ns}
22	—10^{ns}	—11^{ns}	—09^{ns}	—13★	—02^{ns}	06^{ns}
23	06^{ns}	08^{ns}	04^{ns}	05^{ns}	05^{ns}	12★
24	29‡	18†	29‡	16†	06^{ns}	08^{ns}
25	—28‡	—07	—28‡	—03^{ns}	—05^{ns}	—14★
26	11^{ns}	21‡	08^{ns}	21‡	09^{ns}	03^{ns}
27	—02^{ns}	01^{ns}	—02^{ns}	00^{ns}	01^{ns}	08^{ns}
28	09^{ns}	20†	10^{ns}	20†	—02^{ns}	11^{ns}
29	22‡	39§	22‡	36§	03^{ns}	15★
30	38§	46§	32§	44§	27‡	20†
31	22‡	10^{ns}	21‡	08^{ns}	06^{ns}	07^{ns}
32	50§	35§	48§	31§	15★	21‡
33	—39§	—44§	—36§	—41§	—15★	—20†
34	—45§	—52§	—43§	—49§	—15★	—23‡

Boys n = 243   ★ = $p < .05$ § = $p < .0001$

Girls n = 246   † = $p < .01$ ns = not significant

‡ = $p < .001$

Table 4·3 shows the correlations of each of these factors with the criterion, for boys and girls separately; also the correlations of the factors with social class. In most cases it can be seen that the latter are non-significant. A few are highly significant, and these will be discussed presently with regard to their possible importance, even though the partial correlation table has demonstrated that the importance of social class over and above that of the factors is very limited.

Table 4·3 also shows that all of the factors are more closely associated with achievement than they are with social class. This can be interpreted by saying that most of the factors associated with

Table 4.3

Factors which are correlated most highly with the achievement criterion and their correlations with social class

Factor number	Boys	r with social class	Girls	r with social class	Factor number	Boys	r with social class	Girls	r with social class
1	45§	26‡	30§	14★	20	22‡	09	12★	11
2	−22‡	−15★	−27‡	−16★	21	−22‡	−12★	−17★	−11
3	14★	08	32§	11	24	29‡	06	18†	08
4	−14★	−03	−36§	−18†	25	−28‡	−05	−07	−14★
5	20†	08	16†	07	26	11	09	21‡	03
7	−17†	−05	−23‡	−02	28	09	−02	20†	11
8	−09	−09	−23‡	−08	29	22‡	03	39§	15★
9	−21†	05	−20†	−18†	30	38§	27‡	46§	20†
10	34§	23‡	45§	26‡	31	22‡	07	10	07
12	−09	12★	−21‡	−13★	32	50§	15★	35§	21‡
17	09	05	19†	07	33	−39§	−15★	−44§	−20†
19	−21‡	00	−21‡	−10	34	−45§	−15★	−52§	−23‡

Boys n = 243   ★ = p < ·05   ‡ = p < ·001
Girls n = 246   † = p < ·01   § = p < ·0001

achievement in the primary school are not the exclusive characteristic of the middle class. Put another way, we can say that there is more in common between the social classes than there are differences, with respect to factors which are associated with achievement.

The data show that social class correlates with the achievement criterion 0·29 for girls and 0·35 for boys. This means that six factors are more directly important in children's achievement than is social class; for girls, nine factors are more important. These factors are also significantly correlated with social class, and to the extent that this is so these factors suggest some probable reasons why middle-class children are able to achieve well at school. It must be borne in mind though that the correlations are low enough to demonstrate that characteristics which inhibit achievement appear to be present in some middle-class environments, while factors which facilitate achievement are also present in some working-class environments.

Now we shall examine some of the factors which appear so important as antecedents or concomitants of achievement in the primary school, and which at the same time are of greater significance than social class.

Factors which are of greater significance than social class in achievement

Negative factors. For boys and girls alike, six factors come under this category. They were factors 1, 10, 30, 32, 33, and 34. For girls there were three additional factors, 3, 4 and 29. Factors and item loadings are shown in Appendix 4.

The two third order factors are the first to be discussed because they illustrate the kinds of negative conditions in a child's life which can have quite a devastating effect on a child's learning in the primary school. Factor 33 is strongly suggestive of 'Deprivation —cultural, intellectual, social and emotional'. It suggests a child whose parents are too busy to spend time with him (−0·55),[1] or do not share interests or hobbies with him (−0·49), whose behaviour is compared unfavourably with that of other children (−0·42), who gets into trouble if he asks questions (−0·38), whose discussion with parents is restricted (−0·34), whose parents make all the rules and decisions without any reference to the child's opinion (−0·32), whose parents do not make clear the reasons for punishing and make little attempt to understand if he is naughty (−0·33), who finds it difficult to make friends (−0·30), who does not like school (−0·51) or study (−0·48), for whom there is little reading material of interest in his home (−0·30), and in whom there is a strong tendency towards distinct sex role taking, playing with dolls for instance being regarded as specifically for girls (0·35). Factor 33 accounts for 20 per cent of the variance in the criterion of achieve-

[1] Factor loadings of items appear in parentheses. For the factor summary chart, see Appendix 4.

ment for girls, and 14 per cent for boys ($r = 0.44$ and -0.39, $p < .0001$).

Factor 34 is also an inhibitor of learning in the primary school and may be entitled 'Dominant parents, submissive child'. It suggests autocracy and overprotectiveness on the part of the parents, submissiveness on the part of the child and suppressed initiative. The child feels he is too young at the age of eleven to have ideas different from those of the grown-ups in his life (-0.46), his parents are cross every time he attempts to argue with them (-0.43), he is allowed to make few decisions of his own (-0.38), gets into trouble if he tries to find out things for himself (-0.33), likes grown-ups to help him a great deal (-0.36), and is not allowed to take risks (-0.39). This factor on its own accounts for 27 per cent of the variance in the criterion of achievement for girls, and 20 per cent for boys ($= -0.52$ and -0.45, $p < .0001$).

It is of interest that four primary factors were suggestive of autocracy or dominance, factors 2, 12, 13, 22, but they accounted for only 1 to 7 per cent of the variance. When an element of submissiveness on the part of the child was entered into the factor as in factor 34, the amount of variance accounted for leapt from between 1 and 7 per cent up to 20 and 27 per cent, for boys and girls respectively.

Positive factors. From a study of the items which load factor 1, it could be assigned the title 'Academic aspiration and parental support'. The child who scores highly on this factor at age eleven, is already expressing a preference for staying on at school as long as he can to see how far he can go (0.80), and possibly to proceed to university or college in preference to taking a job (0.69). He perceives that he has the support of his parents in these aspirations (0.71) and he enjoys school (0.48). This factor accounts for 20 per cent of the variance in the criterion for boys, and 9 per cent for girls ($r = 0.45$ and 0.30, $p < .0001$).

Factor 10 has been assigned the title 'Strong intellectual and enterprising orientation of child and family', and the highest loading items suggest that looking forward in life the child would prefer a job which offers greater opportunity than security (0.92), where he would have to work 'with his brains' rather than do a manual job

(0·65), his home is a place where interests and hobbies are easy to follow as he wishes (0·37), grown-ups are prepared to spend time with him (0·33), and he is allowed to take physical risks (0·30). Factor 10 accounts for 11 per cent of the variance for boys, and 20 per cent for girls (r = 0·34 and 0·45, p < ·0001).

The next, factor 30, is second order, and has been called 'High level of aspiration and motivation, adjustment with parents, peers and school'. The items suggest that a high scorer prefers to be good at academic work rather than at games (0·56), aspires to higher education rather than a job (0·47), makes little distinction between the accepted behaviour of girls and boys (it matters little if boys play with dolls) (−0·42), interests are shared with parents (0·37), parents think study is important (0·38), he enjoys school and likes to return to school after holidays (0·34), wants to stay at school for a long time and aspires to an important job rather than ease or fame (0·32). For boys factor 30 accounted for 14 per cent of the variance; for girls 21 per cent (r = 0·38 and 0·46, p < ·0001).

Factor 32, another second order factor, 'Intellectual skills, parent support, peer relations not strong', suggests a child who is studious and who feels confident in his ability to learn (0·49), and remember (0·43), who does not spend a great deal of time with peers (−0·41), does not feel that he is compared unfavourably for ability with other children (0·38), enjoys school (0·32), and whose parents do not mind a little argument about some things (0·29). Factor 32 accounts for no less than 25 per cent of the variance in achievement for boys, and 12 per cent for girls (r = 0·50 and 0·35, p < ·0001).

For girls, a further three factors 3, 4 and 29, are more highly significant for achievement than is social class. These three additional factors, therefore, could point to areas which are more critical for girls, probably because they show some of the ways in which families differentiate or discriminate between boys and girls.

Sex differences

Other positive factors. Factor 3, 'Non-indulgent parents', suggests a situation in which the child feels he is not the centre of the home. Parents do not think children are the most important persons in the home (0·76), and are not greatly demonstrative in their affection (0·74), or so it appears to the child. This is a factor of non-indulgence rather than child-centredness; a careful distinction needs to be made between the two. Factor 3 accounts for 10 per cent of the variance in girls' achievement, but only 2 per cent for boys' achievement ($r = 0.32$ and 0.14, $p < .0001$ and $p < .05$).

This finding suggests that girls who are not overindulged do better than those who are. It may also be that those not experiencing a great deal of affection tend to seek compensatory satisfactions in academic endeavour. The factor is not substantial enough to come down on the side of the one interpretation or the other.

Factor 29 is designated 'Independent, free thinking parents and child' because the parents do not appear to insist to their children that they, the parents, know best (0.37), the child is allowed to make his own decisions (0.42), and he feels free to have ideas that are different from those of his parents (0.41), to find out things for himself (0.40), and to choose his own friends in face of parental differences regarding those choices (0.40). Factor 29 accounts for 15 per cent of the variance for girls, and 5 per cent for boys ($r = 0.39$, $p < .0001$ and $r = 0.22$, $p < .001$).

Further negative factors. Factor 4 is clearly one of 'Sex role taking' (choosing an appropriate sex role). The child prefers his own sex role (1.01), has no wishes to be of the opposite sex (0.89), and has a definite idea about what is a suitable kind of play for a boy—'even young boys should not play with dolls' (0.49). There is an inverse correlation between the factor and the achievement criterion ($r = -0.36$ for girls, $p < .0001$ and $r = -0.14$ for boys, $p < .05$), accounting for 12 per cent and 2 per cent of the variance in the criterion for girls and boys respectively. It seems then that for girls, particularly if there is strong sex typing, there is a concomitant lessening in achievement. Perhaps academic achievement is seen by many girls who do poorly as a field of interest more suited for boys. Where the sex roles are seen by children to be less distinct, there appears to be a higher promise of achievement in school.

Factors bearing lesser significant correlations with achievement
Negative factors. The foregoing discussion has been of factors which are more highly correlated with achievement in the primary school than is social class.

The factors now to be discussed were less strong in their association with the achievement criterion than is social class. Some, though not all, of the situations described by these factors are similar to those already discussed.

Factor 2 which has been assigned the description 'Punitive, autocratic parents', correlates negatively with the criterion, −0·22 and −0·27 for boys and girls respectively, and −0·15 with social class. Described in terms of its loadings, this factor suggests a child who feels that punishment is certain if he breaks rules (−0·78), that grown-ups are strict (−0·49), that he is allowed to make few decisions of his own (−0·48), that his choice of friends is dominated by his parents (−0·47), and that there is minimal discussion between him and his parents (−0·34). The correlations (r = −0·22 and −0·27, p < ·001), show that the factor accounts for about 6 per cent of the variance in achievement.

Factor 7 is called 'Uneasy peer relationships,' the children who score highly on this factor experience feelings of loneliness in new company for a long time (−0·68), and feel unable to make friends in a new situation (−0·81 and −0·76). Correlations with achievement are −0·17 (p < ·01), and −0·23, (p < ·001) for boys and girls respectively.

Factor 8, 'Non-sharing of interests between child and parents', is given that title because the loadings suggest that shared hobbies with the father and the mother are restricted if not minimal (−0·85 and −0·35), and interests held in common with them are few (−0·52). The correlation with achievement is −0·9 (ns) for boys and −0·23 (p < ·001) for girls, suggesting that non-sharing of interests between parents and children is more critical for girls than it is for boys.

Factor 9, 'Inferiority and dependence', describes a child who is often told that other children are much cleverer (−0·81), and who likes grown-ups to help him a great deal (−0·60). Correlations are significant for both sexes, −0·21 (p < ·001) for boys and −0·20 (p < ·01) for girls.

Factor 12, 'Thought dominated by parents' suggests that the child who scores highly on this factor feels that his parents think that they know everything best and that children should not have different ideas (−0·95, −0·50). The correlations are −0·09 (ns) and −0·21 (p < ·001) for boys and girls respectively. As with factor 8, girls' performance is more influenced by this factor than boys' performance. The correlations with social class also suggest that girls in working-class families are more dominated than boys, also more than the girls in middle-class families.

Factor 19 is suggestive of 'Identification with adults of opposite sex'. Although only one item loads on the factor, it does load very heavily (−1·00), and deserves to be mentioned. The child who scores highly on this factor considers the work of people of the opposite sex is more interesting than that of his own sex. Considering that by the age of eleven sex typing is usually fairly well advanced, it seems that a high scorer on this factor would not be very well adjusted in his sex role taking, if we are to compare him with the norm. His social relations and aspirations may well be somewhat disordered, and his school performance may then be inferior. The negative correlation −0·21 (p < ·001) for boys and girls alike bears out this hypothesis.

Factor 20 is given the descriptive title 'Unavailability of adults with need for peer relationships' because it suggests that grown-ups are never about when wanted (−0·84), there is minimal sharing of enjoyment between the child and his grown-ups (−0·30), and the child wishes to spend most of his free time with other boys and girls (0·58). In addition there are some feelings of jealousy towards his brothers and sisters. The correlations, −0·22 (p < ·001) and −0·17 (p < ·01) are highly significant.

Factor 25, 'Need for close ties with parents', is so called because the child agrees he would not wish to have a holiday away from his parents (−0·86), he and his parents enjoy many of the same things (0·61). A further item which loads rather weakly on the factor suggests that he lacks confidence in his ability to learn (−0·32). There is clear understanding between the child and his parents regarding the reasons for punishment when administered (0·29). Two of these items suggest a closeness and understanding which almost suggests a lack of autonomy for the child. The correlations, −0·28 (p < ·001) for boys, and −0·07 (ns) for girls, indicate that such close ties are more critical negatively for boys than they are for girls. It could be hypothesized that for girls it is normal to have such close relations with parents, but for boys such closeness is perhaps a symptom of over-dependence beyond the norm, and militates quite strongly against achievement.

Positive Factors. Factor 5 is probably best described as 'Motivation for learning' (Curiosity), and has correlations with achievement of 0·20 for boys and 0·16 for girls (p < ·01). The factor suggests a motivation to explore learning material that is difficult (0·90) and an acceptance of the need for study (0·40).

Factor 17, 'Intellectual skills, concordance of parental and school values' suggests a child who has confidence in his own intellectual skills (0·69 and 0·64) and perceives some coherence between parental values and those of the school (0·42). The correlations with achievement are 0·09 (ns) for boys and 0·19 (p < ·01) for girls.

Factor 20 is described as 'Overprotective parents with independence reaction', the child feeling that his parents are 'far too anxious' about him (−1·09), to which he reacts with a denial that his 'parents know best' (−0·31). Correlations of 0·22 for boys (p < ·001) and 0·12 for girls (p < ·05) are statistically significant. It would seem that it is more the denial of his parents' omnipotence than their overprotectiveness that is instrumental in achievement here, though more research would be required to confirm whether this is true or not.

Factor 24, 'School interests and relationships' is so called because there are high loadings on getting on well with teachers (0·96), preference for academic work over games (0·56), coherence between parents' and teachers' ideas (0·47), confidence in success in school (0·38), and willingness to resume school after the holidays (0·32). The correlations are 0·29 (p < ·001) for boys and 0·18 (p < ·01) for girls.

Factor 26 is a second order factor, and indicates 'Non-striving and ease'. It is difficult to interpret this factor in terms of any psychological theory. A high scorer on this factor would seem to prefer a secure future to one with greater opportunity and less security (−0·46), and comfort and ease rather than responsibility (−0·34). However, one other item which loads quite highly (0·42) suggests coherence between the home and the school concerning which things are important, yet parents do not favour their children having to study to the point of tiredness (-0.30). The low correlation of 0.11 (ns) with achievement for boys is scarcely surprising. However, the correlation for girls is 0.21 ($p < .001$), highly significant. Since both are positively correlated and the significant correlation for girls has to be taken into account, there is a need to consider what explanation can be given for this. It may be that non-strivers do better academically than what Americans somewhat pejoratively call 'grinders'. A more feasible interpretation is that the children who score highly on the factor and yet do well are accustomed to ease because they are bright and have not needed to extend themselves.

Factor 28, another second order factor, is named 'Cultural and intellectual stimulus in an accepting family', because it indicates a home where there is plenty of literature (0.64), where it is easy for hobbies to be pursued (0.45), parents are always ready to answer the child's questions (0.43), and interests are shared between parents and children (0.33), there is no tendency on the part of the parents to compare their children's behaviour unfavourably with that of other children (0.31), and the children feel their parents are reliable and will not let them down (0.31). For boys the correlation of this factor with achievement is 0.09 (ns) and for girls it is 0.20 ($p < .01$). It seems that as with factor 25 this finding suggests that girls are more sensitive than boys to the social context in which they live, and more reliant than boys upon this component in their intellectual development, though this would require more research to be substantiated.

Throughout the discussion of the factors, it will have been noted that factors which affect children's achievement are more critical for girls than for boys. Factors 3, 10, 17, 26, 28, 29 and 30, all having a positive relationship with achievement, and factors, 4, 8, 12, 33 and 34, having negative association lead us to suspect that girls are more sensitive to their environment than boys. They are more field-dependent.

Boys on the other hand are more inner directed and less vulnerable to the limitations imposed by their environment. Also, the roles open to boys appear to be less restricted than for girls. A working-class girl particularly, it appears, is more likely to be 'kept in her place' than a working-class boy, and less likely to have the freedom or initiative to take up roles that are normal for boys.

In the foregoing analysis it has been shown that:

1. Twenty-three factors correlate significantly with achievement; in nearly all instances the correlation of each factor with achievement is higher than the correlation of the factor with social class.
2. Nine factors are more highly correlated with achievement than is social class with achievement.
3. Partialling out social class made only marginal differences to the original product moment correlations between the factors and achievement.

It is therefore concluded that these factors are of greater importance in school achievement than social class itself, and that the characteristics suggested by the factors are not confined to any one social class grouping.

Multiple correlations

The multiple correlation tables again show that the factors are of greater direct importance in achievement than social class. In Tables 4·4 and 4·5 it can be seen that for girls three factors plus family size account for no less than 45 per cent of the variance in achievement. For boys four factors account for 40 per cent of the variance.

The factors which are most highly correlated with achievement have relatively small correlations with social class and it is clear that social class on its own does not have any fundamental importance when compared with the factors. It is interesting to compare the different patterning of factors for the sexes when the data are submitted to multiple correlation. Although, as we have seen in the previous section, most of the factors are of importance in educational achievement for both sexes, there are differences of emphasis. For girls the factors which are of first importance are those which suggest dominance by parents with submissiveness by the child (factor 34, negative relationship), level of aspiration and motivation with adjustment to parents, peers and school (factor 30, positive relationship), family size (negative relationship), hostile contentious parental behaviour accompanied by apparent lack of understanding on their

Table 4.4

Summary table of multiple correlations – all factors – social class excluded – Girls

Step number	Variable entered	Factor number or variable	Multiple correlation	% variance	% increase in variance	r with social class
1	58	34	53	28	28	—123
2	54	30	65	42	14	20
3	7	Family size	66	44	02	11
4	37	13	67	45	01	—05

Table 4.5

Summary table of multiple correlations – all factors – social class excluded – Boys

Step number	Variable entered	Factor number or variable	Multiple correlation	% variance	% increase in variance	r with social class
1	56	32	50	25	25	15
2	27	3	56	31	06	08
3	42	18	60	36	05	17
4	25	1	63	40	04	26
5	15	Worries about the future (growing up)	66	43	03	—10
6	34	10	67	45	02	23

part (factor 13, negative relationship). These four yield a multiple correlation of 0·67, and account for 45 per cent of the variance in educational development as measured by the achievement criterion.

For boys the picture is different, though it must be remembered that this is only a matter of emphasis. The factors which are of first importance before social class are those which suggest confidence in intellectual skills combined with parental support (factor 32, positive relationship), non-indulgence of the child by his parents (factor 3, positive relationship), an apparent tendency for the pupil to regard school work as having intrinsic interest rather than of instrumental value for attaining future success in life (factor 18, positive relationship), and aspiration for educational success and an academic future extending beyond school (factor 1, positive relationship). Together they give a well rounded conceptual view of the nature of motivation which is associated with achievement. These factors produce a multiple correlation of 0·63 and account for 40 per cent of the variance in educational development as measured by the achievement criterion.

The correlations between these factors and social class range from −0·05 to +0·26. Six of the eight do not reach 0·20. It can be seen once again then that the factors most critical in the academic achievement of children are relatively independent of social class. This analysis confirms the partial correlation analysis made earlier.

In both analyses, the factors are seen to have an association with achievement which almost completely overrides that of social class.

These findings are in close agreement with those of Wiseman (1967) in the research which he and his colleagues conducted for the Plowden Committee. The detail and approach of the two studies differ from each other and it is all the more important to note the close agreement. The present research leads to a similar conclusion to that of Wiseman that 'economic level and social class are much less important than aspects of parental attitudes, attitude to education and attitude to books and reading. A high wage packet and a middle-class home does not guarantee a favourable background for educational progress, and literate homes with good parental attitude to school may be found in the slums as well as in the suburbs.' Although social class is clearly of some importance, it is equally clear that the quality of the child's interaction with his environment is of fundamental importance. We should try to take into account the psychological trees when charting the sociological forest.

Anxiety

The review of anxiety studies in Chapter 2 has revealed that the literature of anxiety and achievement is in almost complete disarray. Some researchers have found that high scorers on anxiety scales achieve more highly than low scorers, while others have found the opposite.

It may be that complex learning is adversely affected by anxiety, while learning of simple tasks is enhanced. It may also be that there are too many different measures of anxiety for findings to be consistent.

Without wishing to add to the confusion an attempt was made in this study to discover further knowledge about anxiety and its relation to school performance. To this end a simple inventory of worries which children have was administered to the sample. This inventory is one which has been used by Himmelweit, and also by Bruckman (1964), in previous studies at the London School of Economics. The inventory contains a listing of fifty-two worries which may be experienced by children: worries about growing up (the future), worries about school performance, sensitivity to denigration and rejection by peers, concern with social techniques, appearance and manners, control of temper and language, unwanted feelings of jealousy and selfishness, and relations with parents. The Worries Inventory takes only about ten minutes for a child to complete. The inventory has been factor-analysed by principal component analysis, and a split half reliability test produced a reliability coefficient of 0·88.

In spite of the disagreement between findings on anxiety in other studies (see Lynn, 1956; Hallworth, 1961; Read, 1960) and the methodological difficulties involved in enunciating a satisfactory operational definition of anxiety (see May, 1950), it was still suspected that by using the worries inventory with its component factors of 'anxiety', further light could be thrown on the relation between anxiety and achievement. It was hypothesized that school achievement is more associated with worries about a specific matter (specific anxiety) than with general anxiety. A general worrying attitude, or even specific anxiety about one thing may not have any association with school performance if the child is able to compartmentalize his worries. This hypothesis takes us quite a long way from that wherein general anxiety however defined is supposed to be related to performance. Under the present general hypothesis, that specific anxiety is of greater direct importance than general anxiety, it might be hypothesized that worry about school work would be more strongly associated with performance than general anxiety, assuming a normal population. This study was of a normal population, and not any group which might be encountered in clinical work.

Correlations between total scores on the inventory and the achievement criterion were compared with correlations between specific worries scores (factors) and achievement. These comparisons can be made by reference to Table 4·6.

The table shows that children with a high score on the general worries inventory had a very weak tendency to be low achievers. Correlations of $-0·09$ and $-0·07$ offered some confirmation of the findings of Hallworth (1961) that low achievers have the greater anxiety. But in the present study, although the correlations are in the same direction as those of Hallworth, and although it can be seen that general worries tend to militate against school performance, the correlations are not statistically significant.

By contrast it seems that specific anxiety is of greater consequence in school attainment than general anxiety. The area of anxiety which bore the strongest association with the achievement criterion was one suggestive of worries about growing up and the future; including the thought of leaving school, having to find a job in the future, having to leave home, the thought of marrying. The correlation between this factor and achievement as $-0·25$ for boys, and $-0·23$ for girls ($p < ·001$), both highly significant.

The other areas of anxiety had much lower correlations with the achievement criterion. Nearly zero correlations were found for sensitivity to denigration or rejection by peers, concern with social techniques (manners, appearance), general feelings of guilt, unwanted feelings of selfishness and jealousy, and worries about not being able to control temper. The only other area which bore any significant correlation with the criterion was that suggesting specific worries about school performance, the correlation in this case being $-0·15$ for boys ($p < ·05$), and $-0·11$ for girls (ns). This finding confirms the one reported earlier, that children who are confident of their intellectual skills are more likely to achieve than those who are worried about them, seemingly obvious, yet in contrast to some findings noted in the review of the literature which reported that anxiety can facilitate achievement. The present research has demonstrated a reverse tendency.

Table 4.6

Correlations between worries scores, achievement and social class

Variable	r with VEA		r with social class	
	Boys	*Girls*	*Boys*	*Girls*
Anxiety (worries) – Total Score	—09	—07	—02	02
'Areas of anxiety'				
Growing up	—25‡	—23‡	—11	—09
School Performance	—15*	—11	—05	00
Doing a Good Job	—04	—08	02	—06
Peer Worries (general)	—06	—02	06	04
Sensitivity to denigration	—07	—02	06	00
Rejection by peers	01	06	07	10
Social techniques	—09	—08	00	00
Guilt (general)	—05	02	00	07
Unwanted feelings	—06	06	02	08
Self control	—01	—04	—03	03

n (girls) = 245   n (boys) = 242
* = p < ·05   † = p < ·01   ‡ = p < ·001

In future studies of anxiety and its relation to learning, it would be essential to pin down the problem firmly by taking into account not so much whether children are anxious, but rather what they are specifically anxious about. It would also be necessary to see how this specific anxiety relates to particular learning tasks. The correlations with social class are small if not negligible, and it has not been possible to find any further explanations for social class differences in learning. The factors which have been shown to be associated with learning in the primary school have been more distributed across social class than might have been expected.

5

Summary and conclusions

The aim of this study was to discover some possible explanations for social class differences in primary school achievement and hence educational opportunity. If is often loosely said that the educational system discriminates against working-class children, and there is no shortage of evidence that this is so in some respects. Scores of studies have shown consistently the more general finding that young people of the higher social classes gain the greatest access to educational opportunity at every level. This process starts in the primary years and becomes very much more marked at each stage.

However, it is a distortion to say that the system is to blame entirely for this apparent discrimination against working-class children.

There is relevance in the findings of this study for policy concerning secondary education, in particular the comprehensivation of secondary education. In *All Our Future*, Douglas, Ross and Simpson (1968) stated,

The fact that inequalities existed within the old selective system does not mean that they will disappear when selective examinations are abolished, and the fact that it is the pupils from poor homes who have been handicapped in the past, does not necessarily mean that they will lose their handicaps when comprehensive education becomes universal. Perhaps more rather than less attention will be needed to enable the able boy from a deprived home to use to the full the opportunities offered by his comprehensive school.

This is not an attack on comprehensivation of schools with which the present author is in sympathy. However, it is naïve to imagine that any great reorganization of the school system will automatically cause children and parents who are incapable of taking fullest possible advantage of educational opportunity, to do so. Ultimately greater attention will have to be paid to the motivations which are the product of the home environment, despite the difficulties which are involved.

This research has clearly shown that working-class parents, and indeed some middle-class parents deprive their children of educational opportunity, sometimes in ways of which they can hardly be aware, even where it is their desire to enhance their opportunity. The findings of this study give some indications of ways in which the parent–child interaction can militate severely against children's educational opportunity, and suggests other forms of parent–child interaction which encourage educational progress. The correlations lead one to a limited explanation of social class differences in learning, but they 'explain' more about why some children do well and others do not, *regardless of social class*, than explaining social class differences.

Parental interest in education is of demonstrated importance. It has been further demonstrated in this research that parental interest is multidimensional. The factors discussed earlier are embryonic descriptions of some of these dimensions. If we were actively to set out to cultivate parents' interest in their children's educational opportunity, how might that be done? It would scarcely be enough to tell them that they should be interested. It may be better to try to inculcate in parents habits and attitudes and seek to establish communication patterns between parents and children that will bring about the desired results of improving educational opportunity and achievement among those groups which now deprive themselves of it, be they working-class or middle-class.

The findings of this study show some of the kinds of inculcation which encourage cognitive development in children. There are serious problems involved in any proposal to change people's habits and attitudes, including questions of ethics and feasibility. As to the ethical problems, it is a happy coincidence that those factors which are associated with educational achievement are of such a character that no kind parent would oppose their encouragement. Equally those factors which seem to inhibit achievement are of such a character that it is hard to imagine parents not wanting to eradicate them from the home interaction. To the parent who asks, 'What can I do to help my child achieve better?', there are clear pointers. Broadly they are:

1. Children who gain most educational opportunity tend strongly to come from homes where independent thinking and freedom of discussion among all members is the rule; there are values conducive to intellectual effort and enterprise, and the children's curiosity and academic aspirations are supported and encouraged by parents. The parents do not overindulge them; the children themselves are confident in their intellectual skills (the opposite to being anxious); and they perceive harmony between the values of their home and those of the school.

2. On the negative side, children who gain the least educational opportunity tend strongly to come from homes where their thought is dominated by their parents, and the children themselves accept this as reasonable. There is a climate of general deprivation, with elements of social, cultural, intellectual and emotional deprivation. Parents are punitive and autocratic, and make their children feel inferior to other children. They also tend to overprotect them, yet the children do not feel that their parents are as accessible as they would like them to be. The children also tend to have uneasy peer relationships.

3. Factors which adversely affect educational opportunity and achievement, while more likely to be found in working-class families, are also prevalent in some middle-class families to a greater extent than one would gather from the literature, and than is popularly thought. Most of the influential factors are largely independent of social class.

4. Factors which are positively associated with educational achievement are of such a nature that it would seem that any parent who has his children's interests at heart would regard them as beneficial for their general development. There is a happy congruence here between what a well-disposed parent would prefer for his child and what facilitates academic progress.

5. General 'anxiety' or a disposition to worry about many things has less association with school performance than worries about specific matters. In a normal population, children who are apprehen-

sive about the future are more vulnerable to school failure than children who are not. Worries about the future are more associated with low achievement than are worries about denigration and rejection by peers, lack of confidence in social assets and techniques, unwanted feelings, or guilt and lack of self-control.

6. There are no large sex differences in factors which appear to be critical for educational development. Correlations of all the variables examined are in the same direction for either sex; there are only differences of emphasis, and these are not great.

Girls appear to be slightly more sensitive to their environment than boys. Factors which influence achievement and which reflect the social aspects of the environment affect girls more than boys. Boys on the whole are less subject to the limitations imposed by the environment. They are more inner motivated than girls.

7. Social class remains an important variable in educational opportunity and achievement, but it does not explain anything on its own. If regarded as all important, it can mask factors which are demonstrated to be of greater real importance in understanding differences between children's progress in school. It would certainly appear that the time has arrived for less emphasis on social class itself and more on the discovery of knowledge about the underlying influences.

Implications for educational policy

At the present time in Britain, when educational priority areas (regions where educational opportunity and the ability of children and their parents to take advantage of such facilities as are offered are in a depressed state) are being investigated, it is clearly of importance to make administrative arrangements which encourage an inflow of dedicated people, to make additional finance available for buildings and equipment, and to make every effort to bring home and school together.

However, it seems doubtful if these alone will accomplish all that is hoped or required. It is demonstrably clear that in the last analysis it will be necessary to look beyond broad sociological and physical aspects of the problem, and come to grips with the question of how the one-to-one and group relationships between parents and teachers, children and teachers, and children and parents can be improved. The relationships between parents and children are already determining children's educability well before the end of primary school days, and more likely in the preschool period. These early relationships probably continue to affect learning all through school days and beyond.

Latent educability can very likely be brought out and the wastage of latent ability avoided, not only by providing more and better teachers and buildings, but also by seeking to inculcate, through sophisticated means, improved communication habits and social, cultural and emotional values which are associated with educational development among children and parents. It seems fatuous to cling to the simple idea that the educational system discriminates against the working class, when it can be so clearly seen that there are ways in which some working-class *and* middle-class parents discriminate against their own children, unwittingly, in the matter of educational opportunity. There will, of course, be difficulty in influencing parents who unknowingly discriminate against their children's future life chances to behave in ways which will facilitate them. Some cases will be intractable. Attitudes are not easily changed. But clearly unless some proper attempt is made to educate parents or at least to inform them of facilitating and inhibiting factors that can exist in the family situation, any expenditure incurred in grand reorganizations of the system and on buildings and equipment will achieve less than those tackling the problem would wish.

After the primary school years when children's behaviour patterns and attitudes to education and learning have become set, it becomes less possible to reverse the processes and attitudes that have developed. Anything that can then be done must be no more than an attempted rescue operation. One thing appears to stand out: if educational opportunity is to be maximized, the time to attempt this is not during the secondary school years, but in the primary years if not before.

The failure of children to take advantage of educational opportunity is, in part, a function of low motivation and inability of the children and their parents to see much value in school attendance, or the relevance of it to their own welfare, but more detailed psychological and social factors should not be overlooked when we are considering interest in education and cognitive development.

According to Wall (1955), not infrequently, remedial measures may involve changing the attitudes and behaviour of the family and of the school towards the child. Contacts of this kind are delicate : they require skill and insight which usually come only from specialized training and an objective impartiality, which those personally involved in the child's success or failure may find it difficult to show.

In Mays' (1962) view this task would involve something more constructive than mere liaison and the establishment of support between the teachers and the parents. It would entail positive direction in matters of child care, giving insight to parents regarding the vital phases of child development and the crucial significance of interpersonal relationships in the home.

While enormous budgets are being invested in better buildings and in implementing new forms of school organization, it would seem prudent to invest further comparatively small funds in greater numbers of workers who are properly trained in counselling, guidance and social work, competent to work within a professional relationship with families in seeking to reduce the social and psychological obstacles that make it difficult for so many children to benefit from their educational opportunity.

Suggestions for further research

The following further research is indicated :

1. In seeking to encourage parental 'interest' in their children's cognitive and educational development, it would be useful to conduct research into ways of applying concepts suggested by the factors discovered in this study, together with others whose association with educational achievement has been empirically established. Research should also be carried out to determine the effectiveness of different means of encouraging parental interest.

2. The concepts which have been suggested by the factors should be clarified further and submitted to more empirical research in order to derive well validated and reliable scales for use in clinics and in other research. The factors which appear most deserving of this

kind of refinement are those which suggest the importance of: independent and free thought, communication and action in the family situation (factor 29); deprivation of a many-sided character (factor 33); dominance of parental thought and acceptance of this by the child (factor 34).

3. Other factors arising out of the research were significantly related to the achievement criterion. They were mostly suggestive of academic aspiration, interest in learning, confidence in ability to learn and parental interest and encouragement. These also are worthy of closer attention by researchers, even though their influence may seem more obvious than those which have already been discussed.

4. It seems that studies of anxiety and its association with school performance should be less concerned with general or overall anxiety measures, and should be more concerned with the specific anxieties and worries which children have.

5. In research into social class it must not be so readily assumed as it has been that social class explains differences in educational opportunity and achievement. There should also be more research to identify further factors bearing on academic achievement.

6. Research into language as a determinant of educational success and failure might in future take greater account of the *antecedents of language development* – those non-verbal modes of communication and attitudes between parents and children, which may well lay the foundations for the more complicated speech processes from the earliest years and throughout childhood, particularly as these are perceived by the child.

Appendices

appendices

Appendix I

Development of the inventory by factor analysis

The questionnaire items used in the study were composed with earlier research in child development in mind, particularly the Fels studies and those of Havighurst. Items were invented in consultation with colleagues whose qualifications and experience were in the fields of sociology, psychology and education; each item was designed to probe a particular area.

Whatever pains are taken and whatever the level of psychological sophistication of those framing questionnaire items, *a priori* scales can have only face validity and content validity. It was possible to refine the inventory further by using the method of factor analysis which has the merit of achieving a more parsimonious treatment of the data, at the same time yielding distinct, though embryonic, 'scales' having factorial validity.

Factor analysis and validity

If an instrument is to be valid, it must first satisfy the reliability or internal consistency criterion. In using factor analysis, homogeneity (i.e. the extent to which different parts of the test measure the same thing) and construct or concept validity are built into the 'scales' so derived. Items are assembled in groups according to how highly they correlate with each other,[1] and a functional unity is thus achieved for each factor. There is thus internal consistency and construct validity by definition.

[1] Galton's earlier studies of correlation, of course, are what made 'factors' possible, since factor analysis depends entirely upon correlation procedures. Karl Pearson first described Principal Components in 1901, and Burt simplified these procedures in 1909 (see Burt's *Factors of the Mind*, 1940). I am grateful to Sir Cyril Burt for his efforts towards my greater illumination on the intricacies of factor analysis, its history and development.

Factor analysis, or more correctly 'reference values', was used by Spearman in his early studies of intelligence in which he found formal support for his hypothesis that there is a general factor of intelligence or 'g' (Flugel, 1951). Since then Thurstone (1947) has continued to use the method of factor analysis in his studies and construction of tests of primary abilities, and it is still being used by Cattell and his co-workers in their studies of personality traits (Cattell, 1957).

Factor analysis demonstrates the latent structure of data, the systematic order in which the items cohere and the functional unity which exists between them. A functional unity can be thought of as an underlying variable which accounts for the observed covariance; understanding of such unities is based both on the content of the elements or items involved, and on its relationship to other variables. The factors can be named or identified in terms of the items which load them. These emerging factors or unitary functions have what Cattell (1965) has called construct validity.

Thurstone (1947, p. 51) has drawn an analogy between constructs in natural science and in factor analysis.

The constructs in terms of which natural phenomena are comprehended are man-made inventions. To discover a scientific law is merely to discover that a man-made scheme serves to unify, and thereby to simplify comprehension of a certain class of natural phenomena. A scientific law is not to be thought of as having independent existence. . . . a scientific law is not a part of nature. It is only a way of comprehending nature.

Eysenck (1953), citing Thurstone, added:

The concepts and laws to which factor analysis gives rise are statistical artifacts . . . in the same way that all other scientific concepts and laws are 'artifacts'. Spearman's g (general intelligence) is a statistical artifact to precisely the same extent, and for the same reasons, that Newton's g (gravitational force) was mathematical artifact. Neither has any actual existence . . . both concepts are abstractions which serve to unify and simplify a complex class of phenomena and both had to be discarded or amended when new facts showed them to be incapable of accounting for all the phenomena (p. 109).

The factorial method . . . cannot guarantee the correctness of the causal hypotheses suggested by it [but] ... hypotheses generated by it have proved remarkably accurate when direct experimental test became possible (p. 113).

The advantage of factor analysis is that a large number of apparently discrete meanings are replaced by smaller numbers of conceptual variables. The usefulness of factor analysis in the present study can be realized when it is remembered that a very wide range of family and social variables were being investigated, and that these were thought to be related to each other in some coherent though unknown manner, and by using factor analysis it was possible to bring out the latent structure of the diverse relationships in children's lives at home and school.

Factor analysis establishes the unitary nature of groups of items, arranging them into scales which are homogeneous, self-consistent and clearly distinguishable from each other. Factorial validity and internal consistency are thus established. Factor analysis draws out the hypothetical constructs represented by the several items, and at the same time orders the items in such a way as to show to what extent each item is related to those constructs. An individual person's standing on each factor can also be derived from his responses to items. Each person thus has a certain factor pattern and his responses to the variables making up a factor constitute his factor score.

For more detailed references on factor analysis the reader is referred to Adcock (1954), Cattell (1958), Fruchter (1954), Harman (1960), and Vernon (1949, 1961), Thurstone (1947), Spearman (1927), Guilford (1954), Eysenck (1952a, b, 1953).

The items factor analysed

These are listed in Appendix 4.

The items used in the factor analysis fell into two groups. One in which most of the items concern parents and home, and the other in which most are about school. These were factor analysed to see if embryonic scales could be formed which might be useful in the prediction of academic success of school children.

The data from the closed items in the questionnaire had the most direct relevance to the central problem of the research. The best discriminating items were retained, and seventy-two strongly discriminating items were selected for the factor analysis.

Seventy-two items make a large matrix. From such a large number of good discriminators covering many aspects of social and personality attributes of children, a series of useful factors emerged. It was hoped that a start might be made towards the development of scales that would enable proper replications of the study to be made, and this, together with the desire to make findings having all possible validity, governed the decision to use factor analysis.

The method used

Principal component analysis was used with Varimax orthogonal rotation and Promax oblique rotation. The computer programme used was the F A 5, by Hendricksen and White of the Maudsley Hospital, to whom thanks are due for permission to use it. This programme will accept either raw data or a correlation matrix. It carries out the analysis in three stages (1) Principal Components, or orthogonal unrotated factors, (2) Varimax Rotation for orthogonal simple structure and (3) Promax Rotation for oblique simple structure. The effect of each of these steps is to ensure progressively that, as much as possible, factors will be highly correlated with some of the indices, or items, but uncorrelated with the rest, so as to produce progressively distinctive factors. The two rotation procedures work towards the criterion of 'simple structure' (Thurstone, 1947); this means that few variables load each factor and each variable loads as few factors as possible.

This programme permits any nominated number of factors to be extracted. In this event, second order factors are not extracted. Optionally, as in this study, the Guttman criterion can be used. This means that the number of principal components (and hence primary factors) is determined by the number of latent roots having values above 1·0. Then the programme proceeds to extract higher order factors.

One of the less useful objections to factor analysis is that it cannot yield more than has been put in and that what comes out depends upon what is put in. This is true, of course, of almost anything, not only research, regardless of method used. The advantage of the method used is that it can be used to demonstrate ways in which a large body of data hang together. The patterns, or dimensions which emerge enable further and more precise hypotheses to be made than could be made otherwise, and, if the factors are sufficiently strong and clear-cut, can have direct value for theory and practice.

Appendix 3

The fieldwork

The fieldwork was conducted near the end of the school year after the examinations, before the school excursions which generally are arranged at this time had started.

In conducting research in schools it is essential to choose a time most suitable and convenient for the schools. The beginning of the school year is a time for organizing of classes and time tables, and general settling down. Later in the year preparations for examinations and the examinations themselves are in progress. There is a period in the second term when researchers are more easily allowed access.

For the present research a time was chosen when the examinations were finished: and the results of the selection tests were already available which provided the essential measures of ability and attainment.

No strict time limit was imposed for completion of the questionnaires. It was necessary only to ask the children to do them as quickly and as accurately as they could, and on each occasion the first phase, the large questionnaire on family relations, was completed soon enough to allow time for the anxiety inventory.

As the children finished their papers they were invited to bring them forward. They usually came forward in a gradual flow which gave opportunity to edit carefully. So it was possible to check to ensure that all the required responses had been made. If any were returned uncompleted the children were called out and asked to fill in the outstanding items. Some children were a little shy about an occasional item and a few had not been sure of the meaning. Others were evasive because of mildly felt hostility at being asked the more personal things. But there was no major difficulty as they were assured of confidentiality in answering the items.

Appendix 2

The factors

Question-naire item	Item interpretations	I	2	3	4	5	6	7	8	9	10	11	12	13	14	15	16	17	18	19	20	21	22	23	24	25	26	27	28	29	30	31	32	33	34
																																		Factor loadings	
9	Can remember things easily once learned																	69																	
10	If a thing is hard to learn, becomes interested				90																												43		
11	Wants to stay at school to see how far can go	80																													31				
13	Parents would like child to stay at school until 17 or 18 years old	71																																−35	
14	Parents think much homework should be given											85																							
15	Teachers and parents think the same things are important													30																					
17	Parents and child share many interests																64								47		42								−40
18	Prefers grown ups to help little and encourage own effort					38			−52																				33					−49	
19	Child is seldom told other children are cleverer									−60																							38		−36
21	Chooses own friends in face of parents' disapproval		−41							−81		28										29								40					
22	Feels free to argue with parents a little																						−69	−32	32										
23	Parents always ready to answer child's questions																												43					−38	
24	There are many books at home to interest the child																												64					−30	
25	It is easy to follow hobbies and interests at home												37											−48					45						
28	Is allowed to help parents make rules and decisions													−39																					
29	Parents allow discussion with them on any subject		−34																						−54			−50						−34	
30	Parents do not mind argument on some topics													−34									−77												
32	Child is allowed to make many of own decisions		−48																											42			29		−43
33	If naughty is not spanked		−70																																−38
34	Grownups are not considered by child to be strict		−49																																
35	Is rarely made to feel other children are better behaved													−42															31			34		−42	
36	Can usually get out of punishment after breaking a rule		−78		−27																														
37	Parents generally agree between themselves about rules															−58																			
38	If punished, understands the reason					35																												−34	
39	Does not matter if children and parents quarrel sometimes																						−76			29		−47							
40	Grownups hardly ever quarrel													−42				38	−34																
46	When grownup would prefer responsible job to fame or ease																	−32							30		−34				32				
55	Child thinks parents do not always know best											30				−88					31														
56	Parents do not think they always know best and that children should not differ																												37						
58	At 10 or 11 years children are too young to differ from parents										−95																			41					−46
59	Grownups never let you down										−50																			31					
60	Would never mind having holidays away from parents												1·02																						
61	Parents and child enjoy many of the same things																					−30				−86									
62	Grownups do not seem to be absent too often																					−84				61				37					
63	Grownups are not too busy to spend time with child								33																					39				−30	
65	Wanting to discover things on own does not lead to trouble											31								−29									40					−55	
73	Is confident of high place in class in new school																65								38				35			31			−33
74	If free to choose would like to stay on at school until 18 years old	70																																	
75	Learning is easy																42								−32									−35	
76	Prefers to be good at class work rather than games																								56				56	33					
77	Aspires to university or college	69																											47					−39	
78	Aspires to job mostly using brains, not manual job										29	65																					29	−30	
79	Aspires to job with opportunity, not mere security										92				−31																				
80	Would prefer job requiring thought, not routine																										−46		33						
84	Enjoys school most of the time	48																											34				32		−46
85	Gets on better with teachers than do most children																								96										
88	Good marks in school are of major importance for the future																	−90																	
95	Does not envy grownups not having to study					40																							34					−49	
97	Always glad to start school after holidays																							32			−31		34			−34		−51	
99	Parents do not mind if child studies to tiring point											69													−30				38						
101	Parents think study more important than making money														−61														38						
102	Parents think children most important people at home			−76																															
103	Parents show affection by taking a lot of notice			−74																															
104	Does not feel jealous of siblings													83																					
105	Happy with own lot in family													78								−33													
107	Wishes parents would let him try things out on own					84																									−51				
108	Parents are not over-anxious about child					50																													
109	Does not want to be told how to do everything																				−1·09														
110	Parents allow child to take physical risks			29								30										29						−42		35					−39
111	Parents seldom seem cross													−85																					
112	If naughty, parents always try to understand		−28											−63																				−33	
118	When new anywhere soon makes friends								−81																										
120	Does not take long to make good friends								−76																										−30
121	Cares about peers' opinion																					−47								34					
123	Does not feel lonely in new situations								−68																					34					
124	Likes to spend most of the time with peers																								58					34					
125	Does not envy opposite sex															−32											−30							−41	
126	Prefers life of own sex to opposite sex			89																															
127	Work of own sexed adults is as interesting as that of opposite sex			1·01																											31				
	Thinks even young boys should not play with dolls			49										−30		32			−1·00												31		−42	35	
	Shares hobbies and interests with father								−85																						−30		−36		
	Shares hobbies and interests with mother			−50					−35				−36																	−30					−47

In this table (i) For values of less than 1·00, decimal points have been omitted and all plus signs are omitted
(ii) Negative signs (—) indicate disagreement with items as interpreted.
(iii) Loadings below 0·30 have been omitted in nearly every case.

Subjective reports

As the children finished their questionnaires, they were asked to write on a sheet of paper six sentences under the heading, 'What I thought of the paper.' The purpose of this was fourfold, it helped to prevent boredom, restlessness and disturbance among the children who had finished their papers quickly; allowed the slower ones to feel that they had time to finish without undue haste; gave opportunity for any child who had reacted to the paper with hostility to abreact by expressing his hostile feelings;[1] the written comments of the children could be expected to give a good impression of how genuine their responses to the questionnaire could be taken to be, and how confident they had felt that confidentiality would be preserved. Where hostility had been felt there was no apparent hesitation in stating this. Generally the children wrote that they had enjoyed doing the paper. Some mentioned specifically that they were glad to have been given the opportunity of writing things that they normally could not feel free to say. Many wrote that they would like to do a similar paper again. Of those who were hostile, it was surprising that many were so not because of family secrets being divulged so much as embarrassment about the items concerning other boys and girls, and future job possibilities. The reports suggested a large measure of frankness and willing cooperation on the part of the children. For examples see Appendix 6.

[1] After the fieldwork, checks were made with local education authorities and headmasters of schools and no objections to the papers had come to their notice.

Appendix 4

Factor analysis items

Factor analysis variable	Questionnaire item no.	Item	Scoring
1	9	A Once I learn something, I can remember if I need to	2
		B I seem to forget what I have learnt, just at the time when I need to remember	1
2	10	A If a thing is hard to learn, I get bored with it	1
		B If a thing is hard to learn, I become interested	2
3	11	A The sooner I leave school the happier I shall be	1
		B I want to stay at school and see how far I can get	2
4	13	A I think my parents would like me to stay at school till I am 17 or 18	2
		B I think they would like me to leave school at 15 or 16	1
5	14	A They think children should not have too much homework	1
		B They think quite a lot of homework should be given	2
6	15	A Teachers and parents seem to have different ideas about what is important	1
		B Teachers and parents seem to think the same things are important	2

Factor analysis variable	Questionnaire item no.		Item	Scoring
7	17	A	My parents and I have many interests in common	2
		B	My parents and I have few interests in common	1
8	18	A	I like grownups to help me a great deal	1
		B	I like grownups who want me to do many things on my own and give little help	2
9	19	A	I am hardly ever told that others are much cleverer than I am	2
		B	I am often told how much cleverer other boys and girls are	1
10	21	A	If my parents don't like my friends I see my friends less	1
		B	If they don't like my friends, I still go on seeing my friends as before	2
11	22	A	I feel very uncomfortable when I disagree with my parents	1
		B	It's all right to argue a little with one's parents	2
12	23	A	At home I sometimes get into trouble when I ask questions	1
		B	My parents are very ready to answer all my questions	2
13	24	A	At home there are lots of books which interest me	2
		B	There are not many books at home which interest me	1
14	25	A	It's easy for me to follow any interest or hobby I like at home	2
		B	I would have more interests and hobbies at home, if it were easier to do so	1

Factor analysis variable	Questionnaire item no.	Item	Scoring
15	28	A Sometimes I am asked to help my parents in making rules and deciding things	2
		B They make all the rules and decisions without asking me	1
16	29	A I can talk to my parents about anything —even things they don't like	2
		B There are some things my parents won't let me talk to them about	1
17	30	A My parents do not mind my arguing with them about some things	2
		B They are cross with me every time I argue	1
18	32	A I am allowed to make a lot of my own decisions	2
		B I can make very few decisions of my own	1
19	33	A If I am naughty I generally get a spanking or a hiding	1
		B If I am naughty I do not get spanked	2
20	34	A Grownups are not strict	2
		B Grownups are strict	1
21	35	A I am tired of being told that some other boy or girl is better behaved than I am	1
		B I am hardly ever made to feel that I am less well behaved than any other boy or girl	2
22	36	A If I break a rule I can usually get out of being punished	2
		B Whenever I break a rule I am sure to be punished	1
23	37	A Parents generally agree about rules	2
		B They often disagree about rules	1

Factor analysis variable	Question-naire item no.	Item		Scor-ing
24	38	A	Whenever I am punished I understand clearly why	2
		B	Sometimes I don't understand why I am being punished	1
25	39	A	It does not matter so much if children hear grownups quarrel once in a while	2
		B	It's terribly upsetting when grownups quarrel	1
26	40	A	Grownups hardly ever quarrel	2
		B	Grownups quite often quarrel	1
27	46		When grown up what would you like most?	
			Important job	3
			Be famous	2
			Comfortable easy life	1

			Agree	Not sure	Dis-agree
28	55	Parents always know best	1	2	3
29	56	They always think they know best, and I should not have ideas different from theirs	1	2	3
30	58	Children of 10 or 11 are still too young to have ideas different from those of grownups	1	2	3
31	59	Grownups never let you down	3	2	1
32	60	I would never want to have a holiday away from my parents	1	2	3
33	61	Children and grownups do not enjoy many of the same things	1	2	3

Factor analysis variable	Questionnaire item no.	Item	Scoring Agree	Not sure	Disagree
34	62	Grownups never seem to be about when you want them to be	1	2	3
35	63	They are too busy to spend much time with me	1	2	3
36	65	Wanting to find out things for oneself mostly leads to trouble	1	2	3
37	73	Where do you think you will stand in your class next year when you will be in your new school? Make a guess.	Best 6	Near top 5	One of least 1
38	74	If you were free to do as you liked, at what age would you like to leave school?	At 18 6	At 13 1	
39	75	Learning is	Very hard 1	Very easy 2	
40	76	Which would you rather be? Good at school work, not games 2	Good at games, not school work 1		
41	77	If you were free to choose, which would you prefer when you leave school? Go to university or college 2	Get a job straight away 1		
42	78	When grown up which job would you rather have? Using mostly brains 2	Using mostly hands 1		
43	79	Which of these jobs would you rather have? Get far but might get the sack 2	Get not far, but sure will not get sack 1		

Factor analysis variable	Questionnaire item no.	Item			Scoring
44	80	Which of these jobs would you rather have?			
		Where you have to think things out for yourself			2
		Once you learn it you always know how			1
45	84	How much do you enjoy school?			
		Nearly all the time			3
		Some of the time			2
		I do not like school			1
46	85	How well do you get on with your teachers?			
		Less well than most children			1
		About the same as other children			2
		Better than most children			3
47	88	How important are good marks in school for getting on in the world?			
		Most important of all			4
		Very important			3
		Fairly important			2
		Not very important			1

Factor analysis variable	Questionnaire item no.	Item	Agree	Not sure	Disagree
48	95	Grownups are lucky not having to study	1	2	3
49	97	I'm always glad to start school work after holidays	3	2	1
50	99	My parents think it's bad for children to study so much that they become tired	1	2	3
51	101	My parents think studying more important than making money	3	2	1

Factor analysis variable	Questionnaire item no.	Item	Scoring		
			Agree	Not sure	Disagree
52	102	Parents think children are the most important people at home	3	2	1
53	103	They show they love me by taking a lot of notice of me	3	2	1
54	104	Sometimes I feel jealous of my brother or sister	1	2	3
55	105	I think I have a nicer life than my brother or sister	3	2	1
56	107	I wish they would let me do more things without trying to help me	3	2	1
57	108	They are always far too anxious about me	1	2	3
58	109	I wish they would not always tell me how to do everything	1	2	3
59	110	I am not allowed to take risks in case I get hurt	1	2	3
60	111	They often seem to be cross with me	1	2	3
61	112	If I am naughty they always try to understand	3	2	1
62	118	When I am new anywhere I soon have lots of friends	3	2	1
63	120	It takes a long time to make good friends	1	2	3
64	121	I don't care what other boys/girls think of me	1	2	3
65	123	When I am new anywhere I feel lonely for quite a long time	1	2	3

Factor analysis variable	Question-naire item no.	Item	Agree	Not sure	Dis-agree
				Scoring	
66	124	I like to spend nearly all my time with other boys/girls my age	3	2	1
67	125	Sometimes I wish I were a boy/girl	1	2	3
68	126	Girls } Boys } have a better life than { boys { girls	3	2	1
69	127	The work women/men do is as interesting as that of any man/woman	3	2	1
70	128	Even very young boys should not play with dolls	3	2	1
				No	*Yes*
71	48	Are there hobbies or interests you and your *father* like to do together?		1	2
72	50	Are there any hobbies or interests you and your *mother* like to do together?		1	2

Appendix 5

Items for area scores: 'worries' inventory

The following areas were derived from factors using Principal Component Analysis.

Item

no.   *Area 1.   Worries about growing up (and the future)*

27   The thought of marrying

35   The thought of having to leave school

41   The thought of having to leave home when I am grown up

42   The thought of having to find work later on

47   Finding a job when I am older

Area 2.   Concern about school performance

1   Not doing as well at school as I should like

17   My school work

19   Not being clever enough

23   Not being able to concentrate on my school work

Area 3.   Concern with making a good job of things

1   Not doing as well at school as I should like

5   Starting a thing and then not finishing it

10   Not being good at doing things for myself

23   Not being able to concentrate on my school work

31   Not feeling sure of myself

Area 4.   Relationship with peers
Sub-area 4A.   Sensitivity to denigration by others

38   Girls making fun of me

39   Boys making fun of me

44   Being called names

Item

no.   *Area 4 Relationship with peers—continued*

48   Feeling that some children look down on me

51   Being called stuck-up and stand-offish

Sub-area 4B.   Concern about rejection by others

6   Not getting along well with other children

12   Not being popular

24   Feeling different from other children

32   Feeling left out of things

20   Not feeling at ease with (*a*) boys, (*b*) girls

Sub-area 4C.   Concern with social techniques (self image)

25   The way I talk

3   My looks

4   Not being sure how to behave in company

11   My manners

33   Not knowing how to dress right

Area 5.   Guilt

Sub-area 5A.   Concern about possession of unwanted feelings

46   Having bad thoughts about people I do not like

45   Feeling jealous

40   Not being able to show my parents how much I love them

26   Not helping my parents enough

34   Not doing enough for others

Sub-area 5B.   Concern about control

13   Losing my temper

49   Not telling the truth

8   Using bad language

Area 6.   Parent relations

7   Father not loving me as much as I would like

50   Mother not loving me as much as I would like

52   My parents not understanding me

9   My parents expecting too much of me

28   My parents not being proud of me

Item.

no.   *Area 7. Peer relations (general)*

38   Girls making fun of me

39   Boys making fun of me

44   Being called names

48   Feeling that some children look down on me

51   Being called stuck-up and stand offish

6   Not getting along well with other children

12   Not being popular

24   Feeling different from other children

32   Feeling left out of things

20   Not feeling at ease with (*a*) boys, (*b*) girls

25   The way I talk

3   My looks

4   Not being sure how to behave in company

11   My manners

33   Not knowing how to dress right

Area 8. Guilt (general)

46   Having bad thoughts about people I do not like

45   Feeling jealous

40   Not being able to show my parents how much I love them

26   Not helping my parents enough

34   Not doing enough for others

13   Losing my temper

49   Not telling the truth

8   Using bad language

Area 7 is a composite measure of worries about peers and includes all those items about peers in sub-areas 4*a*, 4*b* and 4*c*.

Area 8 is a composite measure of guilt and includes all those items in sub-areas 5*a* and 5*b*.

Earlier use was made of this inventory in Himmelweit H. T., Oppenheim A. N. and Vince P. (1958) *Television and the Child*. OUP and the Nuffield Foundation.

Appendix 6

Subjective Reports

The following are a selection of typical responses that children made in short notes written after completing questionnaires, in which they were asked to state what they thought of the questionnaires.

1. *Positive reactions*
It was interesting and I think it really made your brain work.
I enjoyed giving my opinion.
I expressed my feelings and thoughts freely without feeling shy.
I thought it was a sensible way to find out such things.
I would like to do another one.
I thought that the paper was quite good. You could speak freely.
It was rather fun to do because you could decide things for yourself.
It was good to define one's personality. Some questions were fun to do, others were rather silly. It was to find out what incipients we have to our future careers and our opinions of ourselves.
(The last was expressed by a boy with a Verbal Ability Quotient 131.)

2. *Objections to items*
The questions were rather embarrassing, but it was good for finding out about the person who did it.
I thought some of the questions were rather personal.
I thought the paper was rather stupid as it pries into people's private lives, but also at the same time it is rather intelligent.
I think it was nosey.
Some sentences were disgraceful and silly, like what you think of marriage and do you like boys.
Some questions were rude, for instance asking what girls thought of boys, and it's none of any bodies business what our fathers work at.

Some questions were rather personal but I managed to answer them without letting too much out.

The one about what you think about girls was quite disgusting. After it was finished I was relieved.

3. *Suggestive evidence of frank responses*

I am glad the teachers are not to see the answers.

If any one else would have seen the answers I would feel rather shy.

I took rather longer than some other children because I pondered a lot.

I am glad Mr Miller and the machine (computer) are the only things to see what I wrote.

It was good because you find out yourself what sort of boy or girl you are.

I could really confess things I would normally not do.

A boy of IQ : 137 : It got down to what *I* thought.

I would not like my parents to see the answers, or my friends, because I would not like them to know what I think of my parents.

4. *Difficulties in completing questionnaires*

A boy of IQ 90 : I thort that ther were a lot of geseyons and thort that it wod tace me ouwer to get thout it. But I got thout it in aboud ¾ of an hower. I diod under stund some of them. uthers I an serd quiet quicly.

The hardest were the continuing sentences (sentence completion).

The hardest question was about what you want to be when you grow up. Another was about where your father works.

It was difficult in some ways because I didn't think I knew, but when I thought I found I did.

Some were awkward but could answer them.

5. *Ease in completing questionnaires*

I thought the paper was very easy.

The paper was just right for the age group 10 to 11.

You found out a lot about us by some simple questions.

It was easy, straightforward and very interesting. I liked the way it was set out and written.

The questions were put in a very good way and were easy to answer.

A boy of IQ 97: It was a long paper but easy. Some of it was funny and the rest was not. It was easy because you answered in your own epinyon. One of the questions was dfft. It was a bit sexy (presumably a reference to the item about getting along with girls).

A boy of IQ 107: it was fairly easy and straightforward. It was a very interesting afternoon with a nice teacher. I liked the questions about our families and hobbies. The printing was nice and clear and I could read every word. It took a long time to do it. It took me about half an hour.

A boy of IQ 78: I thought the paper was very good and I lernt something. On the paper was 132 sentences. It was not very hard. I liked it because it lernt me things.

B stream girl: when I saw the paper and all its pages I thought it would be hard, but I soon found it was easy.

Appendix 7 (a)
Correlation matrix—Girls

Column groups (left to right): Factor numbers | Twenty-five primary factors (1–25) | Seven second order (26–32) | Two-third order (33, 34) | Anxiety and areas (4, 15, 16, 17, 18, 19, 20, 21, 22, 23, 24) | S/class (2) | Family size (7) | s/c school (9) | No. of schools attended (5) | Performance criteria V (10), E (11), A (12) | (VEA) (8) | Factor numbers

Row labels (factor numbers 1–34, then named rows):

Anxiety total score
Growing up
School performance
Doing a good job
Peer worries (general)
Sensitivity to denigration
Rejection by peers
Social techniques (self image)
Guilt (general)
Unwanted feelings
Self control
Conscience

Significance legend:
* p < ·05
† p < ·01
‡ p < ·001
§ p < ·0001

Appendix 7 (b)
Correlation matrix—Boys

Column groups (left to right): Factor numbers | Twenty-five primary factors (1–25) | Seven second order (26–32) | Two-third order (33, 34) | Anxiety and area (4, 15, 16, 17, 18, 19, 20, 21, 22, 23, 24) | S/class (2) | Family size (9) | S/l school (5) | No. of schools attended | Performance criteria V (10), E (11), A (12) | (VEA) (8) | Factor Numbers

Row labels (factor numbers 1–34, then named rows):

Anxiety total score
Growing up
School performance
Doing a good job
Peer worries (general)
Sensitivity to denigration
Rejection by peers
Social techniques (self image)
Guilt (general)
Unwanted feelings
Self control

Significance legend:
* p < ·05
† p < ·01
‡ p < ·001
§ p < ·0001

Part 3

Bibliography

Bibliography

ABRAMS, M. (1964) 'Rewards of education', *New Society*, 9 July 1964.

ADCOCK, C. J. (1954) *Factorial Analysis for Non-mathematicians*, Melbourne University Press.

ALPERT, R. and HABER, R. N. (1960) 'Anxiety in academic achievement situations', *J. abnorm. soc. Psychol.* **61.**

ARVIDSON, G. L. (1956) 'Some factors influencing the achievement of first year secondary modern school children', unpublished Ph.D. thesis, Univ. of London.

AUSUBEL, D. P., SCHIFF, H. A. and GOLDMAN, M. (1953) 'Qualitative characteristics in the learning process associated with anxiety', *J. abnorm. soc. Psychol.* **48.**

AUSUBEL, D. P., SCHIFF, H. A. and ZELENY, M. P. (1953) 'Real life measures of level of academic and vocational aspiration in adolescents : relation to laboratory measures and to adjustment', *Child Dev.* **24,** 3 and 4.

BALDWIN, A. L. (1955) *Behaviour and Development in Childhood*, New York, Dryden.

BALDWIN, A., KALHORN, J. and BREESE, F. (1949) 'The appraisal of parent behaviour', *Psychol. Monogr.* **63,** 4.

BENDIG, A. W. (1960) 'Extraversion, neuroticism and student achievement in introductory psychology', *J. educ. Res.* **53.**

BENE, E. (1957) 'The objective use of a projective technique, illustrated by a study of the differences in attitudes between pupils of grammar school and of secondary modern schools', *Brit. J. educ. Psychol.* **27.**

BERLYNE, D. E. (1957) 'Recent developments in Piaget's work', *Brit. J. educ. Psychol.* **27.**

BERNSTEIN, B. (1958) 'Some sociological determinants of perception', *Brit. J. Sociol.* **9.**

BERNSTEIN, B. (1960) 'Language and social class', *Brit. J. Sociol.* **11.**

BIGGS, J. B. (1959) 'The teaching of mathematics, 2 : Attitudes to arithmetic—Number anxiety', *Educ. Res.* **1,** 3.

BINET, A. (1909) *Les Idées moderne sur les enfants*, Paris, Flammarion; cited in Hunt (1961).

BLALOCK, H. M. (1960) *Social Statistics*, McGraw-Hill.

BLOMQVIST, J. (1956a) *Studies Related to Failure in School in Sweden*, University of Stockholm, Research Bulletin of Institute of Education, no. 7.

BLOMQVIST, J. (1956b) 'Betyg och Studieframgång', *Folkskoll Årarnas Tidning*.

BLOMQVIST, J. (1958) *Kvarsittning Och Skolframgang*, Stockholm, Almqvist and Wiksell (with an English summary).

BOSSIO, V. (1965) 'Language development and reading attainment in deprived children', in M. L. Kellmer Pringle (1965), Deprivation and Education. Longmans.

BOWLBY, J. (1952) *Maternal Care and Mental Health*, Geneva, WHO.

BOYLE, E. (1963) Foreword to the Newsom Report, *Half Our Future*, see Central Advisory Council for Education.

BOYLE, E. (1964) 'The Conservative essence', *New Society*, 8 Oct. 1964.

BRIMER, M. A. (1956) 'The relationship between ability and attainment—a suggested revision of current theory', *Bull. Nat. Found. Educ. Res.*, **8**.

BROADBENT, D. E. (1958) *Perception and Communication*, Pergamon.

BRONFENBRENNER, U. (1958) Socialisation and social class through time and space, in E. E. Maccoby, T. M. Newcomb and E. L. Hartley, *Readings in Social Psychology*, 3rd edn. Holt, 1958.

BRUCKMAN, I. R. (1964) 'Social and psychological variables associated with need achievement in primary school children', unpublished Ph.D thesis, University of London.

BURNS, C. L. C. (1949) 'Maladjusted children of high intelligence', *Brit J. educ. Psychol.* **19**.

BURT, C. (1921) *Mental and Scholastic Tests*, Staples.

BURT, C. (1925) *The Young Delinquent*, University of London Press.

BURT, C. (1937) *The Backward Child*, University of London Press.

BURT, C. (1941) *The Factors of the Mind; an introduction to factor analysis in psychology*, New York, Macmillan.

BURT, C. (1944) *The Young Delinquent*, 4th edn, University of London Press.

BURT, C. (1947) 'Symposium on selection for secondary schools', *Brit. J. educ. Psychol*, **17**.

BURT, C. (1955) 'Evidence for the concept of intelligence', *Brit. J. educ. Psychol.* **25**, pt iii.

BURT, C. (1965) Letters to Times Educational Supplement, 17/9/65.

BURT, C. and HOWARD, M. (1952) 'The nature and cause of maladjustment among children of school age', *Brit. J. Psychol. Stat.*, **5**, pt 1.

BURT, C. and HOWARD, M. (1957) 'Heredity and intelligence—a reply to criticisms', *Brit. J. statist. Psychol.* **10**, pt 1.

BURT, C. and SCHONELL, F. J. *et al.* (1957) 'The relationship between ability and attainment', *Bull. Nat. Found. Educ. Res.* **9**.

BUSWELL, M. M. (1953) 'The relationship between the social structure of the classroom and the academic success of the pupils', *J. exp. Educ.* **22**.

CAMPBELL, W. J. (1951) 'Sociocultural environment and educational progress, unpublished Ph.D. thesis. University of London.

CASTENADA, A., PALERMO, D. S. *and* MCCANDLESS, B. R. (1956) 'Complex learning and performance as a function of anxiety and task difficulty', *Child Development*, **72**.

CASTLE, E. B. (1965) *Ancient Education and Today*, Penguin (Pelican).

CATTELL, R. B. (1948) *A Guide to Mental Testing*, University of London Press.

CATTELL, R. B. (1957) *Personality and Motivation Structure and Measurement*, Harcourt, Brace.

CATTELL, R. B. (1958) *Personality and Motivation Structure and Measurement*, Harrap.

CATTELL, R. B. (1965) *Scientific Study of Personality*, Penguin (Pelican).

CATTELL, R. B. and BUTCHER, J. (1965) *The Prediction of Achievement and Creativity*, Bobbs Merrill.

CATTELL, R. B. and SEALY, A. P. (1965) *The General Relations of Changes in Personality and Interest to Changes in School Performance: An exploratory study*; Report to the Office of Education on Co-operative Research, Project no. 1411, Laboratory of Personality Assessment, University of Illinois.

CATTELL, R. B., SEALY, A. P. and SWENEY, A. B. (1966) 'What can personality and motivation source traits measurements add to the prediction of school achievement?' *Brit. J. Educ. Psychol.* **36**, 3.

CENTRAL ADVISORY COUNCIL FOR EDUCATION (1954) *Early Leaving*, HMSO.

CENTRAL ADVISORY COUNCIL FOR EDUCATION. *Half Our Future* (Newsom Report), HMSO, 1963.

CENTRAL ADVISORY COUNCIL FOR EDUCATION, *Children and Their Primary Schools* (Plowden Report), HMSO, 1967. Vol 2 : Research and Surveys, App. 8 by A. T. Collis, G. W. Miller and J. Parker, and App. 9 by S. Wiseman.

CHAMBERLAIN, A. F. (1900) *The Child: a study in the evolution of man*, Scribners, cited in H. Bakwin, (1941) 'Emotional deprivation in infants'. *J. Pediat.* **35**.

CHAMPAIGN COMMUNITY UNIT SCHOOLS, Dept of Special Services Staff, (Champaign, Illinois) (1961) 'Factors associated with under achievement and over achievement of intellectually gifted children, *Except. Children*, **28**.

CHAMPNEY, A. (1941) 'The variables of parent behaviour', *J. Abnorm. and Soc. Psych.* **36.**

CHANSKY, N. M. (1958) 'Threat, anxiety and reading behaviour', *J. educ. Res.* **51.**

CHILD, I. L. (1954) 'Personality', *Ann. Rev. Psychol.* **5.**

Children and their Primary Schools, See CENTRAL ADVISORY COUNCIL FOR EDUCATION, 1967.

CLARK, R. A., TEEVAN, R. and RICCIUTI, H. N. (1956) 'Hope of success and fear of failure as aspects of need for achievement', *J. abnorm. soc. Psychol.* **53.**

COLEMAN, J. S. (1959) 'Academic achievement and the structure of competition', *Harv. educ. Rev.* **29.**

COLLIS, A. T. (1967) *Children and their Primary Schools*, see *Central Advisory Council for Education*.

CONKLIN, A. M. (1940) 'Failure of highly intelligent pupils', *Teach. Coll. Contrib. Educ.*, 792. Cited in Morrow and Wilson (1961).

COX, F. N. (1956) 'Social stimulation, anxiety level and learning efficiency : a theoretical analysis', *Aust. J. Psychol.* **8.**

CRAFT, M., RAYNOR, J. and COHEN, L., eds., *Linking Home and School*, Longmans, 1967.

CRANDALL, V. (1964) 'Parents' attitudes and behaviours and grade school children's academic attainments', *J. genet. Psychol.* **104.**

CRANE, A. R. (1959) 'An historical and critical account of the accomplishment quotient idea', *Brit. J. educ. Psychol.* **29.**

CRONBACH, L. J. (1949) *Essentials of Psychological Testing*, Harper.

CROSLAND, A. R. (1962) *The Conservative Enemy*, Cape.

CURETON, E. E. (1937) 'The accomplishment quotient technic', *J. exp. Educ.* **5.**

DAVIS, A. (1944) 'Socialisation and adolescent personality'. *Chicago Nat. Soc. for Study of Education, 43rd Yearbook.*

DAVIS, A. (1947) 'Socialisation and adolescent personality', in T. M. Newcomb and E. L. Hartley eds (1947) *Readings in Social Psychology*. Holt.

DAVIS, A. (1948) *Social Class Influences upon Learning*, Harvard University Press.

DAVIS, A. and HAVIGHURST, R. J. (1952) 'Social class and colour differences in child rearing, in G. Swanson, T. M. Newcomb and E. L. Hartley eds, *Readings in Social Psychology*, Holt, 1952.

DOLLARD, J. and MILLER, N. E. (1945) *Social Learning and Imitation*, Routledge and Kegan Paul.

DOLLARD, J. and MILLER, N. E. (1950) *Personality and Psychotherapy*, McGraw-Hill.

DOUGLAS, J. W. B. (1964) *The Home and the School*. McGibbon & Kee.

DOUGLAS, J. W. B. (1967) *The Home and the School*. Panther.

DOUGLAS, J. W. B., ROSS, J. M. and SIMPSON, H. R. (1969) *All Our Future*, Peter Davies.

DUFF, O. L. and SIEGEL, L. (1960) Biographical factors associated with academic over- and under-achievement. *J. educ. Psychol.* **51**.

EASTERBROOK, J. A. (1959) 'The effect of emotion on cue utilisation and the organisation of behaviour', *Psychol. Rev.* **66**.

EDUCATION COMMITTEE'S YEARBOOK, Association of Education Committees.

EDUCATION (1957) Editorial, cited by Crane (1959).

EDUCATIONAL TESTING SERVICE ANNUAL REPORT 1965–66, Princeton, ETS.

ELDER, G. H. (1963) 'Parental power legitimation and its effect on the adolescent', *Sociometry*, **26**.

ELDER, G. H. (1965) 'Family structure and educational attainment', *Amer. sociol. Rev.*, **30**, 1.

ENTWISTLE, N. J. and CUNNINGHAM, S. (1968) 'Neuroticism and School Achievement. A linear Relationship?' *Brit. J. educ. Psychol.* **38**.

ERIKSON, E. (1950a) *Childhood and Society*, New York, Norton.

ERIKSON, E. (1950b) 'Growth and crises of the "Healthy personality",' in M. J. E. Senn, ed. *The Healthy Personality*, New York, Macy, 1950.

EYSENCK, H. J. (1952a) *The Scientific Study of Personality*, Routledge and Kegan Paul.

EYSENCK, H. J. (1952b) 'Uses and abuses of factor analysis', *Appl. Statistics*, **1**.

EYSENCK, H. J. (1953) 'The logical basis of factor analysis, *Amer. Psychologist*, **8**.

EYSENCK, H. J. (1957) *The Dynamics of Anxiety and Hysteria*, Routledge and Kegan Paul.

EYSENCK, H. J. (1959) *Manual of the Maudsley Personality Inventory*, London ULP.

EYSENCK, H. J. and COOKSON, D. (1969) 'Personality in Primary School Children, *Brit J. educ. Psychol.* **39**, 2.

FARBER, I. E. and SPENCE, K. W. (1953) 'Complex learning and conditioning as a function of anxiety', *J. exp. Psychol.* **45**.

FERREIRA, J. R. and OAKES, P. W. (1960) 'Automatic data processing; an aid in studying pupil characteristics', *Calif. J. educ. Res.*, **11**, cited in *Psychol. Abstr.* (1960).

FLOUD, J. (1963) 'Teaching in the affluent society', in *Yearbook of Education*, Evans.

FLOUD, J. (1964) 'Education and social class', in *New Society*, 20 February 1964.

FLOUD, J. and HALSEY, A. H. (1957) 'Intelligence Tests, social class and selection for secondary schools', *Brit. J. Sociol.* **8**.

FLOUD, J., HALSEY, A. H. and MARTIN, F. M. (1956) *Social Class and Educational Opportunity*, Heinemann, pp. 148–9.

FLUGEL, J. C. (1951) *A Hundred Years of Psychology*, Duckworth.

FOULDS, G. A. and CAINE, T. M. (1965) *Personality and Personal Illness*. Tavistock.

FRANCE, N. (1963) 'The relationship between primary and secondary school success: a six year follow-up study in a large administrative area', unpublished Ph.D. thesis, University of London.

FRANKEL, E. (1960) 'A comparative study of achieving and underachieving high school boys of high intellectual ability', *J. educ. Res.* **53**.

FRASER, E. D. (1955) Social factors in school progress, unpublished Ph.D. thesis, Aberdeen University.

FRASER, E. D. (1959) *Home Environment and the School*, University of London Press.

FREEBURG, N. E. and PAYNE, D. T. (1967) 'Parental influence on cognitive development in early childhood: a review', *Child Dev.* **38**, 1.

FREUD, A. (1936) *The Ego and the Mechanisms of Defence*, New York, International UP.

FREUD, S. (1915) 'Repression', in *Collected Papers*, 4. Hogarth Press, 1946.

FREUD, S. (1923) *The Ego and the Id*, Hogarth Press, 1947.

FREUD, S. (1926) *Inhibitions, Symptoms and Anxiety*, Hogarth Press, 1948.

FREUD, S. (1936) *The Problem of Anxiety*, trans. H. A. Bunker, Norton.

FREUD, S. (1960) *A General Introduction to Psychoanalysis*, New York, Washington Square.

FRUCHTER, B. A. (1954) *Factor Analysis*, Van Nostrand.

FURNEAUX, W. D. (1956) *Report to Imperial College of Science and Technology*, cited in Lynn and Gordon (1961).

FURNEAUX, W. D. (1961) *The Chosen Few*, Oxford University Press.

GETZELLS, J. W. and JACKSON, P. W. (1960) 'The study of giftedness: a multi-dimensional approach', *The Gifted Student*, Cooperative Research Monograph (no 2), Washington, U.S. Office of Education, cited in De Haan and Havighurst (1961).

GETZELLS, J. W. and JACKSON, P. W. (1962) *Creativity and Intelligence: exploration with gifted students*, Wiley.

GLASS, D. V. (1964) Introduction to Douglas (1964).

GLASS, D. V. *et al*. (1954) *Social Mobility in Britain*, Routledge & Kegan Paul.

GOLDFARB, W. (1943) 'The effects of early institutional care on adolescent personality', *J. exp. Educ.* **12**.

GOLDFARB, W. (1945) 'Effects of psychological deprivation in infancy and subsequent stimulation', *Amer. J. Psychiat.* **102**.

GORDON, E. A. (1958) 'Self esteem, need for achievement, test anxiety and performance', Doctoral dissertation, Yale University, cited in Waite *et al*. (1958).

GOUGH, H. G. (1946) 'The relationship of socio-economic status to personality inventory and achievement test scores.' *J. educ. Psychol.* **37.**

GRANT, N. (1964) *Soviet Education*, Penguin (Pelican).

GRIFFITHS, S. R. (1962) 'The attitudes towards school of pupils in junior, secondary modern and secondary grammar schools with special reference to effects of selection at 11 plus', unpublished M.A. thesis, University of London.

GROOMS, R. R. and ENDLER, N. S. (1960) 'The effect of anxiety on academic achievement', *J. educ. Psychol.* **51.**

GUILFORD, J. P. (1950) 'Creativity', *Amer. Psychologist*, **5.**

GUILFORD, J. P. (1954) *Psychometric Methods*, 2nd edn, McGraw-Hill.

GUILFORD, J. P. and LACEY, J. I. (1947) *Printed Classification Tests*, Army Air Forces Aviat. Psychol. Prog. Res. Rep. no. 5, Washington D.C.

GYNTHER, R. A. (1957) 'The effects of anxiety and of situational stress on communicative efficiency', *J. abnorm. soc. Psychol.* **54.**

HAAN, R. F. DE and HAVIGHURST, R. J. (1961) *Educating Gifted Children*, 2nd edn, University of Chicago.

HAGGARD, E. A. (1957) 'Socialisation, personality and academic achievement in gifted children', *School Rev.* **65,** 4.

HALLWORTH, H. J. (1961) 'Anxiety in secondary modern and grammar school children', *Brit. J. educ. Psychol.* **31**

HALSEY, A. H. (1958) 'Genetics, social structure and intelligence', *Brit. J. Sociol.* **9.**

HALSEY, A. H. and GARDNER, L. (1953) 'Selection for secondary education and achievement in grammar schools', *Brit. J. Sociol.* **4.**

HARMAN, H. H. (1960) *Modern Factor Analysis*, University of Chicago.

HART, B. and SPEARMAN, C. (1912) 'General ability—its existence and nature, *Brit. J. Psychol.* **5.**

HARTUP, W. W. and ZOOK, E. A. (1960) 'Sex role preferences in three- and four-year old children', *J. consult. Psychol.* **24.**

HATTWICK, B. W. and STOWELL, M. (1936) 'The relation of parental over-attentiveness to children's work habits and social adjustments in kindergarten and the first six grades of school', *J. educ. Res.* **30.**

HAVIGHURST, R. J. (1953) *Human Development and Education*. Longmans.

HAVIGHURST, R. J., BOWMAN, P. H., LIDDLE, G., MATTHEWS, C. and PIERCE, J. (1962) *Growing Up in River City*, Wiley.

HEBB, D. O. (1949) *The Organisation of Behaviour*, Wiley.

HEBB, D. O. (1958) *A Textbook of Psychology*, W. B. Saunders.

HIMMELWEIT, H. T. (1954) 'Social status and secondary education since the 1944 Act : some data for London', in Glass (1954).

HIMMELWEIT, H. T. (1955) 'Socio-economic background and personality', *Int. soc. sci. Bull.* **7.**

HIMMELWEIT, H. T. (1960) 'Social class differences in parent child relations in England', *Research Papers in Family Sociology*, UNESCO.

HIMMELWEIT, H. T. (1965) 'Folie d'Examen and university entrance', *Times Educational Supplement*, 10 September 1965.

HIMMELWEIT, H. T. and WHITFIELD, J. W. (1949) 'Mean intelligence scores of a random sample of occupations', *Brit. J. Industr. Med.* **1.**

HIMMELWEIT, H. T., OPPENHEIM, A. N. and HALSEY, A. H. (1952) 'The views of adolescents on some aspects of the social class structure', *Brit. J. Sociol.* **3.**

HINDLEY, C. B. (1962) 'Social class influence on the development of ability in the first five years. *Child Education*, eds. A. G. Skard and T. Husén, Copenhagen, Munksgaard, cited in Young (1965).

HINDLEY, C. B. (1965) 'Stability and change in abilities up to five years; group trends', *J. child Psychiat.* **6.**

HORA, H. (1956) 'A study of the relationship between educational failure and early maternal deprivation in primary school children of average intelligence', unpublished Ph.D. thesis, University of London.

HORNEY, K. (1937) *The Neurotic Personality of Our Time*, New York, Norton.

HOTYAT, F. et al. (1947) *Niveau d' Instruction Primaire en Hainaut*, cited in Wall et al. (1962).

HUNT, J. MCV. (1961) *Intelligence and Experience*, New York, Ronald.

HUSÉN, T. (1966) 'The relation between selectivity and social class in secondary education', *Int. J. educ. Sci.* **1**, 1.

JACKSON, B. and MARSDEN, D. (1962) *Education and the Working Class,* Routledge & Kegan Paul.

JACKSON, R. W. B. and FERGUSON, G. A. (1941) 'Studies on the reliability of tests', *Bull. Dept. educ. Res., Toronto Univ.,* **12**.

JAHODA, G. (1951) 'A study of the chief social determinants of occupational choice in secondary school leavers, with special reference to social class factors and level of aspiration', unpublished Ph.D. thesis, University of London.

JAYASURIA, D. L. (1960) 'A study of adolescent ambition, level of aspiration and achievement motivation', unpublished Ph.D. thesis, University of of London.

JINKS, P. C. (1964) 'An investigation into the effect of date of birth on subsequent school performance', *Educ. Research,* **6**, 3.

JOHN, V. P. (1963) 'The intellectual development of slum children : some preliminary findings', *Amer. J. Orthopsychiat.* **33**, 5.

JONES, E. S. (1955) 'The probation student : what he is like and what can be done about it', *J. educ. Res.* **49**.

KAGAN, J. (1956) 'The child's perception of the parent', *J. abnorm. soc. Psychol.* **53**.

KAGAN, J. and LEMKIN, J. (1960) 'The child's differential perception of parental attributes', *J. abnorm. soc. Psychol.* **61**.

KAGAN, J. and MOSS, H. A. (1962) *Birth to Maturity: a study in psychological development,* Wiley.

KAGAN, J., HOSKEN, B. and WATSON, S. (1961) 'The child's symbolic conceptualisation of the parents', *Child Dev.* **32**.

KAGAN, J., SONTAG, L. W., BAKER, C. T. and NELSON, V. L, (1955) 'Personality and IQ change', *J. abnorm. soc. Psychol.* **56**.

KELLER, S. (1963) 'The social world of the urban slum child : some early findings', *Amer. J. Orthopsychiat.* **33** 5.

KELSALL, R. K. (1957) *Report of an Enquiry into Applications for Admission to Universities,* Association of Universities of the British Commonwealth.

KEMP, L. C. D. (1954) 'An investigation into environmental and other characteristics determining the attainment of children in a group of London primary schools', unpublished Ph.D. thesis, University of London.

KEMP, L. C. D. (1955) 'Environmental and other characteristics determining attainment in primary schools', *Brit. J. educ. Psychol.* **25**.

KIM, Y., ANDERSON, H. E. and BASHAW, W. L. (1968) 'Social maturity, achievement, and basic ability', *Educ. and Psychol. Dev.* **28.**

KIMBALL, B. (1953) 'Case studies of educational failure during adolescence', *Amer. J. Orthopsychiat.* **23.**

KLAUSMEIER, H. J. (1958) 'Physical, behavioural and other characteristics of high and low achieving children in favoured environments', *J. educ. Res.* **51.**

KURTZ, J. L. and SWENSON, E. J. (1951) 'Factors related to overachievement and underachievement in school', *School Rev.* **59,** 8.

LANTZ, B. (1945) 'Some dynamic aspects of success and failure', *Psychol. Monogr.* **59,** 1, cited in Pressey, Robinson and Horrocks (1959).

LAWTON, D. (1968) *Social Class, Language and Education*, Routledge and Kegan Paul.

LEVY, D. M. (1933) 'Relation of maternal overprotection to school grades and intelligence tests', *Amer. J. Orthopsychiat.* **3.**

LYNN, R. (1955) 'Personality factors in reading achievement', *Proc. Roy. Soc. Med.* **48.**

LYNN, R. (1956) 'The relation of anxiety to educational attainment in school children', unpublished Ph.D. thesis, Cambridge University, cited in Hallworth (1961).

LYNN, R. (1957) 'Temperamental characteristics related to disparity of attainment in reading and arithmetic', *Brit. J. educ. Psychol.* **27.**

LYNN, R. (1959) 'Two personality characteristics related to academic achievement', *Brit. J. educ. Psychol.* **29.**

LYNN, R. and GORDON, I. E. (1961) 'The relation of neuroticism and extraversion to intelligence and educational attainment', *Brit. J. educ. Psychol.* **31.**

MAAS, I. (1955) 'Psychological aspects of class differences and child upbringing', unpublished M.A. thesis, University of London.

MCCANDLESS, B. R. and CASTENADA, A. (1956) 'Anxiety in children, school achievement and intelligence', *Child Dev.* **27.**

MCCLELLAND, D. C., ATKINSON, J. W., CLARK, R. A. and LOWELL, E. L. (1953) *The Achievement Motive*, Appleton Century Crofts.

MACCOBY, E. E. and GIBBS, P. K. (1954) 'Methods of child rearing in two classes', in W. E. Martin and C. B. Stendler, eds, *Readings in Child Development*, Harcourt, Brace.

MADDOX, H. (1957) 'Nature-nurture balance sheets', *Brit. J. educ. Psychol.* **27.**

MANDLER, G. and SARASON, S. B. (1952) 'A study of anxiety and learning', *J. abnorm. soc. Psychol.* **47.**

MARTIN, W. E. and STENDLER, C. B., eds. (1954) *Readings in Child Psychology*, Harcourt, Brace.

MASLOW, A. H. (1943) 'A theory of human motivation', *Psychol. Rev.* **50**.

MAY, R. (1950) *The Meaning of Anxiety*, Ronald.

MAYS, J. B. (1962) *Education and the Urban Child*, Liverpool University Press.

MILLER, G. W. (1967) See Central Advisory Council for Education, *Children and Their Primary Schools*.

MILLER, G. W. (1970) 'Factors in School Achievement and Social Class', *J. educ. Psychol.* **61**, 4.

MILLER, N. E. (1951) 'Learnable drives and rewards', in S. Stevens, *Handbook of Experimental Psychology*, Wiley.

MILLER, N. E. and DOLLARD, J. (1941) *Social Learning and Imitation*, Yale University Press.

MOBERG, S. (1951) 'Vem blev student och vad blev studentem', Ph.D. thesis, Lund, cited by Husén (1966).

MOLDAWSKY, S. and MOLDAWSKY, P. C. (1952) 'Digit span as an anxiety indicator', *J. consult. Psychol.* **16**.

MONTGOMERY, K. (1956) 'An enquiry into the relationship between early school leaving and attitude toward authority figures', Ed.D. Dissertation, Michigan State University, cited in *Dissert. Abstr.* **16**, 901.

MORGAN, J. J. B. and BANKER, M. H. (1938) 'The relation of mental stamina to parental protection', *J. genet. Psychol.* **52**.

MORRISON, A. and MCINTYRE, D. (1969) *Teachers and Teaching*, Penguin.

MORROW, W. R. and WILSON, R. C. (1961a) 'Family relations of bright high-achieving and under-achieving high school boys', *Child Develpm.* **32**.

MORROW, W. R. and WILSON, R. C. (1961b) 'The self reported personal and social adjustment of bright high-achieving and under-achieving high school boys', *J. child. Psychol. Psychiat.* **2**, cited in *Psychol. Abstr.* **36**.

MOWRER, O. H. (1950) *Learning Theory and Personality Dynamics*. Ronald.

MULLIGAN, R. A. (1951) 'Socio-economic background and college enrollment', *Amer. sociol. Rev.* **16**.

MUNDY, L. (1957) 'Environment and intellectual function', *Brit. J. med. Psychol.* **30**.

NEWMAN, H. H., FREEMAN, F. N. and HOLZINGER, K. J. (1937) *Twins: a study of heredity and environment*, University of Chicago Press.

Newsom Report, see *Central Advisory Council for Education*.

OPPENHEIM, A. N. (1956) 'A study of social attitudes of Adolescents'. Unpublished Ph.D. thesis, University of London.

OTTAWAY, A. K. C. (1962) *Education and Society*, Routledge & Kegan Paul.

Educational opportunity and the home

PARKER, J. (1967) See Central Advisory Council for Education, *Children and Their Primary Schools*.

PECK, R. F. and HAVIGHURST, R. J. (1960) *The Psychology of Character Development*, Wiley.

PEPPIN, B. H. (1963) 'Parental understanding, parental acceptance and the self concept of children as a function of academic over- and under-achievement', unpublished Ph.D. thesis, Claremont Graduate School, cited in *Dissert. Abstr.* 23.

PETERS, R. S. (1965) *Authority, Responsibility and Education*, Allen & Unwin.

PIAGET, J. (1947) *The Psychology of Intelligence*, trans. M. Piercey and D. E. Berlyne, Routledge & Kegan Paul.

PIAGET, J. (1952) *The Origins of Intelligence in Children*, trans. M. Cook, International Universities Press.

PIAGET, J. (1953) *The Origins of Intelligence in the Child*, Routledge & Kegan Paul.

PIDGEON, D. A. (1957) 'Ability and attainment—a further note', *Bull. Nat. Found. educ. Res.* 10.

PIDGEON, D. A. (1964) 'Date of birth and scholastic performance', *Educ. Research*, 7.

PIDGEON, D. A., YATES, A. and BRIMER, M. A. (1957) 'Ability and attainment', *Bull. Nat. Found. educ. Res.* 9.

PIDGEON, D. A., YATES, A., BRIMER, M. A. and MORRIS, B. (1956) 'The relationship between ability and attainment', *Bull. Nat. Found. educ. Res.* 8.

Plowden Report, see *Central Advisory Council for Education*.

PORTER, J. F. (1957) A sociological investigation into causes of early leaving of children from grammar school', unpublished M.A. thesis, University of London.

PRESSEY, S. L., ROBINSON, F. P. and HORROCKS, J. E. (1959) *Psychology in Education*, Harper.

PRIESTLEY, R. R. (1957) 'The mental health of university students', *Melbourne Studies in Education*, Melbourne University Press.

RANK, O. (1929) *The Trauma of Birth*, Harcourt, Brace.

RAO, K. U. (1954) 'The effects of stress on level of aspiration behaviour', unpublished Ph.D. thesis, University of London.

REED, H. B. (1960) 'Anxiety—the ambivalent variable', *Harv. educ. Rev.* 30, 2.

RIBBLE, M. (1943) *The Rights of Infants*, Columbia University Press.

RIBBLE, M. (1944) 'Infantile experience in relation to personality development', in J. McV. Hunt, ed. *Personality and the Behaviour Disorders,*

RICKARD, G. (1954) 'The relationship between parental behaviour and children's achievement behaviour', Doctoral dissertation, Harvard University, cited in Morrow and Wilson (1961).

RIESSMAN, F. (1960) 'Workers' attitudes towards participation and leadership', unpublished Ph. D. thesis, Columbia University, cited in Riessman (1962).

RIESSMAN, F. (1962) *The Culturally Deprived Child,* Harper & Row.

ROBINOWITZ, R. (1956) 'Attributes of pupils achieving beyond their level of expectancy', *J. Pers.* **24.**

ROE, ANN (1953) *The Making of a Scientist.* Dodd Mead.

ROFF, M. A. (1949) 'A factorial study of the Fels parent behaviour scales', *Child Dev.* **20.**

ROSEN, B. C. (1956) 'The achievement syndrome: a psycho-cultural dimension of social stratification', *Amer. sociol. Rev.* **21.**

ROSEN, B. C. (1959) 'Race, ethnicity and the achievement syndrome', *Amer. sociol. Rev.* **24.**

ROSEN, B. C. and d'ANDRADE, R. (1959) 'The psycho-social origins of achievement motivation', *Sociometry,* **22.**

ROUCEK, J. S. (1965) 'The role of educational institutions with special reference to highly industrialised areas', in *The Education Explosion, The World Yearbook of Education,* Evans.

SANDIN, A. A. (1944) 'Social and emotional adjustments of regularly promoted and non-promoted pupils', *Teach. Coll. Ch. Devt. Monogr.,* **32,** cited in Pressey *et al.* (1959).

SARASON, S. B., DAVIDSON, K., LIGHTHALL, F. and WAITE, R. (1958) 'Class room observation of high and low anxious children', *Child Dev.* **29.**

SARNOFF, I., SARASON, S. B., LIGHTHALL, F. and DAVIDSON, K. S. (1959) 'Test anxiety and the eleven-plus examination', *Brit. J. educ. Psychol.* **29.**

SCHACHTER, S. (1963) 'Birth order, eminence and higher education', *Amer. sociol. Rev.* **28,** 5.

SCHOEPPE, A., HAGGARD, E. A. and HAVIGHURST, R. J. (1953) 'Some factors affecting 16-year-olds' success in five developmental tasks', *J. abnorm. soc. Psychol.* **48.**

SCHONELL, F. J. (1956) 'School failure', in *The Slow Learning Child* 3, University of Queensland Press.

SCHONELL, F. J., ROE, E. and MEDDLETON, I. G. (1962) *Promise and Performance: A Study of Student Progress at University Level,* University of London Press.

SCOTTISH COUNCIL FOR RESEARCH IN EDUCATION (1957) *The Trend of Scottish Intelligence*, University of London Press.

SEALY, A. P. and CATTELL, R. B. (1964) *Changes Over a Junior High School Year in the Relation of Achievement to Ability, Personality and Interest*, U.S. Dept. of Health, Education and Welfare.

SHAW, M. C. and DUTTON, B. E. (1962) 'The use of a parent attitude research inventory with the parents of bright academic under-achievers', *J. educ. Psychol.* **53.**

SHAW, M. C. and MCCUEN, J. T. (1960) 'The onset of academic under-achievement in bright children', *J. educ. Psychol.* **51.**

SHERMAN, M. and BELL, E. (1951) 'The measurement of frustration: an experiment in group frustration', *Personality*, *1*, cited in Pressey *et al.* (1959).

SHOUKSMITH, G. and TAYLOR, J. W. (1964) 'The effect of counselling on the achievement of high ability pupils', *Brit. J. educ. Psychol.* **34.**

SINGER, M. B. (1961) 'A study of children of high intelligence with relatively low school achievement', unpublished Ph.D. thesis, University of London.

SKEELS, H. M. and DYE, H. B. (1939) 'A study of the effects of differential social stimulation on mentally retarded children. *Proc. Amer. Assoc. ment. Def.* **44,** cited in Hunt J. McV. (1961).

SMYKAL, A. (1962) 'A comparative investigation of home environmental variables related to achieving and under-achieving behaviour of academically able high school students', *Dissert. Abstr.* **23,** 1.

SPEARMAN, C. (1927) *The Abilities of Man*, Macmillan.

SPIELBERGER, C. D., GOODSTEIN, L. D. and DAHLSTROM, W. G. (1958) 'Complex incidental learning as a function of anxiety and task difficulty', *J. exp. Psychol.* **56.**

SPIRO, M. (1958) *Children of the Kibbutz*, Harvard University Press.

SPITZ, R. A. (1945) 'Hospitalism: an inquiry into the genesis of psychiatric conditions in early childhood', in *The Psychoanalytic Study of the Child*, *1*, New York, International Universities Press.

SPITZ, R. A. and WOLF, K. M. (1946) 'Anaclitic depression: an inquiry into the genesis of psychiatric conditions in early childhood, 2.' in *The Psychoanalytic study of the child*, *2*. International Universities Press.

STAGNER, R. (1948) *Psychology and Personality*, McGraw-Hill.

STOTT, D. H. (1950) 'Causal factors in the delinquencies of boys committed to an approved school', unpublished Ph.D. thesis, University of London.

STRODTBECK, F. L. (1958) 'Family Interaction, Values and Achievement' in D. C. McClelland, ed. *Talent and Society*, Van Nostrand.

SULLIVAN, H. S. (1947) *Conceptions of Modern Psychiatry*, Washington, W. A. White Foundation.

SUTTON, R. (1961) 'An analysis of factors related to educational achievement', *J. genet. Psychol.* **98**.

SYMONDS, P. M. (1947) 'The sentence completion test as a projective technique', *J. abnorm. soc. Psychol.* **42**.

TAKANO, S. (1959) 'An experimental study of children's behaviour in failure', *Jap. J. educ. Psychol.* **7**, cited in *Psychol. Abstr.* **35**.

TANNER, J. M (1961) *Education and Physical Growth*, Evans.

TERMAN, L. M. and ODEN, M. H. (1948) *The Gifted Child Grows Up*, Oxford University Press.

TERMAN, L. M. and TYLER, L. E. (1954) 'Psychological sex differences', in L. Carmichael ed, *Manual of Child Psychology*, Wiley.

THURSTONE, L. L. (1938) *Primary Mental Abilities*, University of Chicago Press.

THURSTONE, L. L. (1944) 'A factorial study of perception' *Psychometr. Monogr.* No. 4.

THURSTONE, L. L. (1945) 'The effects of selection in factor analysis', *Psychometrika*, **10**.

THURSTONE, L. L. (1947) 'Psychological implication of factor analysis', *Psychometric Lab. Rep.* no. 44.

THURSTONE, L. L. (1947) *Multiple Factor Analysis*, University of Chicago Press.

TIBBETTS, J. R. (1955) 'The role of parent child relationships in the achievement of high school pupils', Ph.D. thesis, New York University, cited in *Dissert. Abstr.* **15**.

TODD, F. J., TERRELL, G. and FRANK, C. E. (1962) 'Differences between normal and underachievers of superior ability', *J. appl. Psychol.* **46**.

VERNON, P. E. (1940) *The Measurement of Abilities*, University of London Press.

VERNON, P. E. (1949) *Measurement of Abilities*, University of London Press.

VERNON, P. E. (1953) *Personality Tests and Assessments*, Methuen.

VERNON, P. E. (1957) *Secondary School Selection*, Methuen.

VERNON, P. E. (1958) 'The relation of intelligence to educational backwardness, *Educ. Rev.* **11**.

VERNON, P. E. (1960) *Intelligence and Attainment Tests*, University of London Press.

VERNON, P. E. (1961) *Structure of Human Abilities*, Methuen.

VERNON, P. E. (1963) 'The Pool of ability', in P. Halmos, *Sociological Research Monograph no. 7*. Keele.

VERNON, P. E. (1958) 'A new look at intelligence testing', *Educ. Res.* 1, 1.

WAITE, R. R., SARASON, S. B., LIGHTHALL, F. F. and DAVIDSON, K. S. (1958) 'A study of anxiety and learning in children', *J. abnorm. soc. Psychol.* 57.

WALL, W. D. (1955) 'Education and Mental Health', UNESCO *Problems in Education*, 11.

WALL, W. D., SCHONELL, F. J. and OLSEN, WILLARD C. (1962) *Failure in School*, Hamburg, UNESCO Institute for Education.

WALSH, A. M. (1956) *Self Concepts of Bright Boys with Learning Difficulties*, Columbia University Press.

WARNER, W. L., HAVIGHURST, R. J. and LOEB, M. B. (1944) *Who Shall Be Educated?* Harper.

WARREN, J. R. and HEIST, P. A. (1960) 'Personality attributes of gifted college students', *Science*, 132.

WHITE, R. W. (1959) 'Motivation reconsidered, the concept of competence', *Psych. Rev.* 66, 5.

WHITEHEAD, A. N. (1933) *Science and the Modern World*, Cambridge University Press, p. 126.

WILSON, R. C., GUILFORD, J. P., CHRISTENSEN, P. R. and LEWIS, D. J. (1954) 'A factor analytic study of creative thinking abilities', *Psychometrika*, 19.

WINTERBOTTOM, M. R. (1953) 'The relation of childhood training in independence to achievement motivation', Ph.D. thesis, University of Michigan, cited in *Dissert. Abstr.* 13, and in Rosen (1956).

WISEMAN, S. (1964a) *Education and Environment*, Manchester University Press.

WISEMAN, S. (1964b) 'In Defence of IQ tests', *New Society*, 21 May 1964.

WISEMAN, S. (1967) See Central Advisory Council for Education, *Children and Their Primary Schools*.

YATES, A. and PIDGEON, D. A. (1957) *Admission to Grammar Schools*, Newnes.

YOUNG, M. (1965) *Innovation and Research in Education*, Routledge & Kegan Paul.

Index

Index